SPELLING
Grade 2

Table of Contents

SPELLING
Grade 2

Credits:
School Specialty Publishing Editorial/Production Team
Vincent F. Douglas, B.S. and M. Ed.
Tracey E. Dils
Jennifer Blashkiw Pawley
Teresa A. Domnauer
Tracy R. Paulus
Suzanne M. Diehm

Big Tuna Trading Company Art/Editorial/Production Team
Mercer Mayer
John R. Sansevere
Erica Farber
Brian MacMullen
Matthew Rossetti

Send all inquiries to: School Specialty Publishing, 8720 Orion Place, Columbus OH 43240-2111

ISBN 1-57768-832-5

6 7 8 9 10 11 QPD 09 08 07 06 05

WELCOME TO CRITTERVILLE!

Spider

Frog

Grasshopper

Mouse

Little Critter

Little Sister

Dad

Kitty

Mom

Blue

Gator

Bat Child

Gabby

Bun Bun

Tiger

Maurice

Molly

Malcolm

Spelling the Short a Sound

Eyes and Ears

Sound	Sign	Spelling
short **a**	/a/	m**a**p h**a**t

Say each word. Listen for the short **a** sound in **map** and **hat**.

Study the spelling. How is the short **a** vowel spelled?

Write the words.
1-10. Write the ten words. Circle the letter that spells the short vowel sound.

Word List

lap

nap

hat

map

has

pat

mad

gas

fat

bad

1. l@p

2. _____

3. _____

4. _____

5. _____

6. _____

7. _____

8. _____

9. _____

10. _____

Spelling Tip
The short **a** sound is often spelled **a**.

Words You Know

Complete the story with the correct words from the word list.

A Day with Grandpa

Grandpa _____ a small farm. I like to sit on his _____ and hear stories.

One day, Grandpa took me for a ride. First, we put _____ in the car. Then, Grandpa read the _____. Grandpa forgot his _____. He wasn't _____. He gave me a _____ on the back. I ran to get Grandpa's hat. I almost tripped over Grandpa's _____cat! The cat was taking a _____ on the floor.

It's too _____ we were running late. We only went for a short ride.

Word Fun: Word Families

Change the first letter in each word to spell a word from the word list. Write the words.

1. bat _____

2. cap _____

3. cat _____

4. lad _____

Words You Know

Fill in the Letters: Write the two words from the word list that fit each puzzle.

1-2.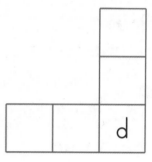

3-4.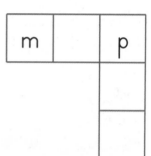

5-6.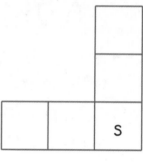

7-8.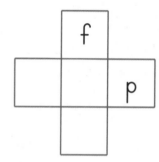

Unscramble and Spell: Write a word from the word list by changing the order of the following letters.

9. ash _____

10. pal _____

11. tap _____

12. pan _____

Pair Up the Words: Write the missing word that goes with each word.

13. good and _____

14. coat and _____

15. oil and _____

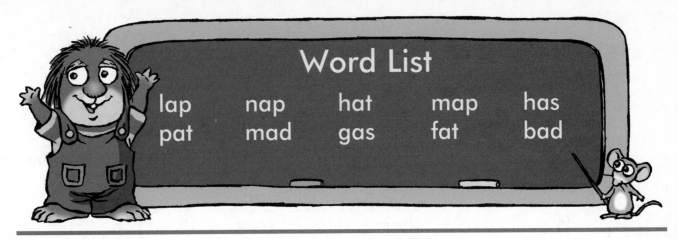

Word List

lap	nap	hat	map	has
pat	mad	gas	fat	bad

Proofreading Practice

Here is Little Critter's story about a bad day. Circle the three words that are spelled wrong. Write each word correctly in the spaces below.

> Monday was a bed day. I spilled milk on my lup. After that I sat on my new hat. Then I could not find the state I live in on the mep. I was sad that day.

1. _____ 2. _____ 3. _____

Review

Write a word from the word list for each clue below.

4. It makes a car run. _____

5. You wear this on your head. _____

6. You can find your town on this. _____

Spelling the Short i Sound

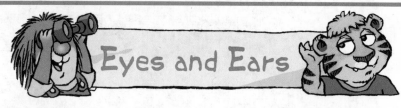

Eyes and Ears

Sound	Sign	Spelling	
short i	/i/	pin	fix

Word List

- if
- fix
- pin
- his
- mix
- rip
- kiss
- hid
- tip
- milk

Say each word. Listen for the short i sound in **pin** and **fix**.

Study the spelling. How is the short vowel spelled?

Write the words.
1-10. Write the ten words. Circle the letter that spells the short vowel sound.

1. ⓘf   6. _____
2. _____ 7. _____
3. _____ 8. _____
4. _____ 9. _____
5. _____ 10. _____

Spelling Tip
The short i sound is often spelled i.

Complete the story with the correct words from the word list.

A Real Treat

Gator loves _____ mom. He wanted to do something that would make her happy. So he went into the kitchen to _____ her lunch.

Gator had to do many things to get ready. He had to _____ off the leaves from a head of lettuce. Next, he cut off the _____ of a carrot. Then he had to _____ the cooked vegetables. Finally, he poured her a glass of _____.

When Gator was finished, he tried to _____ a flower on his mom's napkin. Then he _____ a note under her dish. His mom gave him a big _____.

Could you make lunch _____ you tried?

Word Fun: Opposites

Write the opposite of each word. Each answer will have a short i sound.

1. her _____   3. break _____   5. out _____

2. small _____   4. stand _____

Words You Know

Look and Write: Write the words from the word list that fit each clue.

Two words that end with the letter x.

1. _____   2. _____

Two words that end with two consonants.

3. _____   4. _____

The word that has the word in in it.

5. _____

Two words that rhyme with lip.

6. _____   7. _____

Swap a Vowel: Change the vowel in each word in the table below to make a word from the word list. Write the word below.

8. tap	9. has	10. of	11. had	12. fox

Use the Dictionary: Words in a dictionary are arranged in ABC order. Look at the first letter in each word below. Write the word in each group that would come first in ABC order.

13. rip   pin   mix _____   15. rip   milk   kiss _____

14. hid   tip   if _____   16. milk   if   pin _____

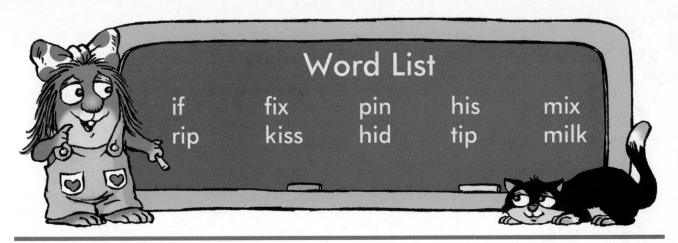

Word List

if	fix	pin	his	mix
rip	kiss	hid	tip	milk

Proofreading Practice

Here is Gator's list. Circle the words that are spelled wrong. Write each word correctly in the spaces below.

1. Fex a broken toy ef I can.

2. Play a game.

3. Give Mom a hug and a kis.

1. _____ 2. _____ 3. _____

 # Review

Write a word from the word list that fits each group of words.

4. hug, wave, hello, good-bye, _____

5. juice, water, tea, _____

6. hers, yours, mine, theirs, _____

Spelling the /o/ and /ô/ Sounds

Eyes and Ears

Sound	Sign	Spelling
short o	/o/	job
	/ô/	log

Say each word. Listen for the vowel sounds in job and log. Note the sign for each sound.

Study the spelling. How are these sounds spelled?

Write the words.
1-10. Write the ten words. Circle the letter that spells the vowel sound.

Word List

log
got
dog
job
lot
fog
flop
spot
jog
off

1. l(o)g
2. _____
3. _____
4. _____
5. _____
6. _____
7. _____
8. _____
9. _____
10. _____

Spelling Tip
The short o and /ô/ sounds are often spelled o.

Words You Know

Complete the story with the correct words from the word list.

Gabby's Job

Gabby has a new _____ after school. She _____ the job last week. Gabby is happy because she will now be able to save some money. She wants to buy some new pet fish.

Gabby's job is a _____ of fun. She takes a big black and white _____ for walks. She has to take the dog out every day in sun, rain, or _____.

Sometimes Gabby takes the dog to a safe _____ and runs around with it. Other times she sits by herself on a _____ while the dog runs _____ by itself. Maybe one day she will _____ with the dog. Then they both will _____ down under a tree to rest.

Word Fun: More Than One

Add -s to each word to show more than one.

1. one log, two _____

2. one spot, two _____

3. one pot, two _____

4. one hog, two _____

5. one frog, two _____

6. one tot, two _____

Words You Know

Listen and Write: Write the word from the word list that has the same ending sound as the picture words. Circle the word that ends with two consonants.

 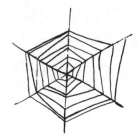 

1. _____ 2. _____ 3. _____

Rhyme and Answer: Write the missing word. It will rhyme with the underlined word.

4. A place for a bed is a <u>cot</u> _____.

5. A wooden toy for a pet is a <u>dog</u> _____.

6. A yard for children is a <u>tot</u> _____.

Add Another Word: Think how the words in each group are alike. Write the word from the word list that belongs in each group.

7. snow, sleet, rain, _____

8. fish, cat, bird, _____

9. walk, skip, run, _____

10. hot, spot, lot, _____

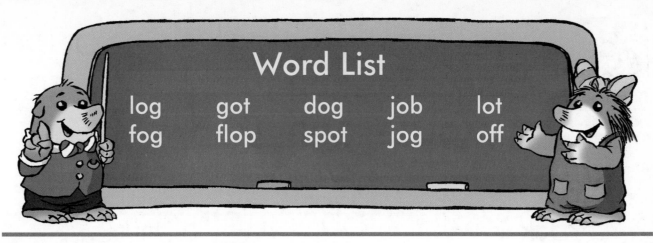

Word List

log	got	dog	job	lot
fog	flop	spot	jog	off

Proofreading Practice

Here is Little Critter's letter. Circle the three words that are spelled wrong. Write each word correctly in the spaces below.

Dear Grandma and Grandpa,

    I got a jeb It is a lat of work. I wash our dog.

I get off every spat of dirt My family likes my work.

So does my dog.

                  Love,

                  Little Critter

1. _____ 2. _____ 3. _____

4 - 5. Two periods are missing. Correct the mistakes.

Review

Write a word from the word list to complete each sentence. The missing word will rhyme with the underlined word.

6. An oven or fire is a <u>hot</u> _____.

7. A pig who "barks" is a <u>hog</u> _____.

8. When you have a little, you do <u>not</u> have a _____.

Spelling the Final /k/ Sound

Eyes and Ears

Sound	Spelling
/k/	lo**ck**

Word List

rock

kick

sack

dock

pack

sick

stack

lock

stick

snack

Say each word. Listen for the last sound you hear in **lock**.

Study the spelling. How is this sound spelled?

Write the words.
1-10. Write the ten words. Circle the letters that spell the last sound.

1. r o (ck)   6. _____

2. _____   7. _____

3. _____   8. _____

4. _____   9. _____

5. _____   10. _____

Spelling Tip
A final /k/ sound
is spelled **ck**.

Words You Know

Complete the story with the correct words from the word list.

A Busy Afternoon

Today I will go down to the boat _____ with my friend, Tiger. There is a lot of trash on the dock. People should put their trash in the garbage. All the cans left around make me _____! We will _____ them in a pile and take them to the dump.

Later we can _____ a ball around the yard. Then we can climb to the top of the big _____. We will _____ on apples and nuts. Tiger and I will _____ the food in a bag. I will carry the paper _____ in my backpack. I will bring a long _____ to help me walk. I hope I will not forget to _____ my house door before I go.

Word Fun: Word Meaning

Write the word from the word list that means the same or almost the same as each word.

1. pole _____

2. bag _____

3. stone _____

4. pile _____

5. ill _____

6. treat _____

Words You Know

Change Numbers to Letters: Use the code below to help you write six words from the word list.

Number	1	2	3	4	5	6	7	8	9	10
Code	a	c	d	i	k	l	o	p	s	t

1. 6-7-2-5 _____

2. 9-4-2-5 _____

3. 9-10-4-2-5 _____

4. 5-4-2-5 _____

5. 9-10-1-2-5 _____

6. 8-1-2-5 _____

Read and Write: Write the words from the word list that fit each clue.

Three words that begin with two consonants.

7. _____   8. _____   9. _____

Four words that have a short a sound.

10. _____ 11. _____ 12. _____ 13. _____

Three words that have a short o sound.

14. _____   15. _____   16. _____

Two words that begin like stop.

17. _____   18. _____

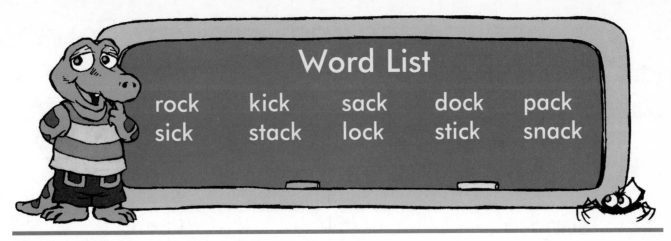

Word List

rock	kick	sack	dock	pack
sick	stack	lock	stick	snack

Proofreading Practice

Here is Tiger's list. Circle the three words that are spelled wrong. Write each word correctly in the spaces below.

Things I Like to Do

1. Kik a football.

2. Hit a ball with a stik.

3. Fish off the dok.

4. Climb a rock.

1. _____ 2. _____ 3. _____

Review

Write a word from the word list to complete each sentence.

4. Grandma doesn't feel well. She feels _____.

5. The best after school _____ is an apple.

6. Maurice put one block on top of the other.

   He made a _____.

Spelling the /nd/ and /st/ Sounds

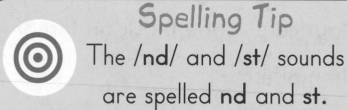

Eyes and Ears

Sound	Spelling
/nd/	ha**nd**
/st/	lo**st**

Word List

sand

pond

lost

just

and

last

list

band

fast

hand

Say each word. Listen for the last sound your hear in **hand** and **lost**.

Study the spelling. How are these sounds spelled?

Write the words.
1-10. Write the ten words. Circle the letters that spell the last sound.

1. __sa nd__   6. _____

2. _____   7. _____

3. _____   8. _____

4. _____   9. _____

5. _____   10. _____

Spelling Tip

The /nd/ and /st/ sounds are spelled **nd** and **st**.

Complete the story with the correct words from the word list.

My Lost Cat

Fluffy is my pet cat. I cannot find her anywhere. She is
_____. I saw her _____ this morning after breakfast.
Fluffy and I were near the frog _____ in my backyard. I
was digging in the _____. She was sitting next to me
looking around.

I held out my _____. "Here, Fluffy!" I called. But
she ran away as _____ as she could. Maybe she saw
another cat or a dog or a mouse! That was the _____
time I saw her.

She has a white _____ around her neck. She has
white paws _____ a white tail.
I made a _____ of places to
look for her. I hope that I will
find her soon. I miss my pet!

Word Fun: Words That Describe

Write the words from the word list that the describing words tell
something about.

1. big, loud _____

2. hot, white _____

3. left, right _____

4. deep, small _____

Words You Know

Make New Words: Take the first two letters and the last two letters of each word to make a word from the word list. For example: <u>sa</u>lt + wi<u>nd</u> = sand

1. pool + land _____
2. life + mist _____
3. love + fist _____

4. hall + kind _____
5. fair + rust _____

Listen to the Sounds: Write the word from the word list that begins with the same sound as each picture.

6. _____

8. _____

10. _____

7. _____

9. _____

Keep Looking: Write the word from the word list that you find in each of these words.

11. unjust _____
12. breakfast _____
13. grand _____

14. listless _____
15. everlasting _____

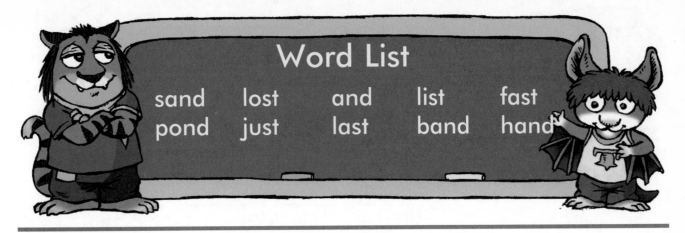

Word List

sand	lost	and	list	fast
pond	just	last	band	hand

Proofreading Practice

Here is Gabby's poster. Circle the three words that are spelled wrong. Write each word correctly in the spaces below.

PLEASE HELP!

Have you seen Toby He is lawst. He is a brown and white horse. He has a white bandd down his back. Toby was last seen near the pend.

1. _____   2. _____   3. _____

4. One question mark is missing at the end of a question. Correct the mistake.

Review

Write a word from the word list that is the opposite of each word below.

5. found   _____

6. first   _____

7. slow   _____

Spelling the Short e Sound

Eyes and Ears

Sound	Sign	Spelling
short e	/e/	fed

Say each word. Listen for the short e sound in **fed**.

Study the spelling. How is the vowel sound spelled?

Write the words.
1-10. Write the ten words. Circle the letter that spells the short e sound.

Word List

egg
fed
met
them
rest
bend
yet
test
went
send

1. ⓔgg

2. _____

3. _____

4. _____

5. _____

6. _____

7. _____

8. _____

9. _____

10. _____

Spelling Tip
The short e sound is
often spelled e.

Complete Little Critter's letter with the correct words from the word list.

Dear Grandma and Grandpa

Dear Grandma and Grandpa,

The other day I watched a robin build a nest. After the mother bird sat on it awhile, a tiny _____ hatched. The baby robin poked its head out and _____ its mother.

The mother robin did not sit and _____. She _____ away to find food. Then she came back and _____ the baby a worm. She had to _____ way down to feed it.

Of course, the baby robin cannot leave the nest _____. Some day it will _____ its wings and try to fly.

I drew a picture of _____. I will _____ it to you. Will you come here soon to see the robins and their nest?

Love,
Little Critter

Word Fun: Past Tense

Add **-ed** to each word to show the past.
Now I **pick**. A day ago I **picked**.

1. rest _____   4. rent _____

2. test _____   5. peck _____

3. spell _____

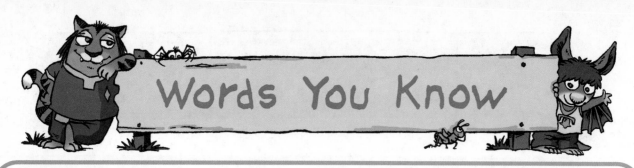

Words You Know

Spell the Shapes: Use each of the shapes to help you spell the words. Circle the three words that end with two consonants.

● = r   ▲ = m   ■ = h   ∪ = s

■ = t   ↑ = n   ◆ = d   ↓ = e

1. ▲↓■ _____

2. ■↓∪■ _____

3. ∪↓↑◆ _____

4. ■■↓▲ _____

5. ●↓∪■ _____

Use the Dictionary: Where would you look to find these six words in the dictionary? Use the chart below to help you.

went   met   egg   fed   yet   bend

abcdefghi	jklmnopq	rstuvwxyz
look in the beginning of the dictionary	look in the middle of the dictionary	look at the end of the dictionary

6. Which three words are found at the beginning of the dictionary?

_____   _____   _____

7. Which word is found in the middle?

_____

8. Which two words are found at the end of the dictionary?

_____   _____

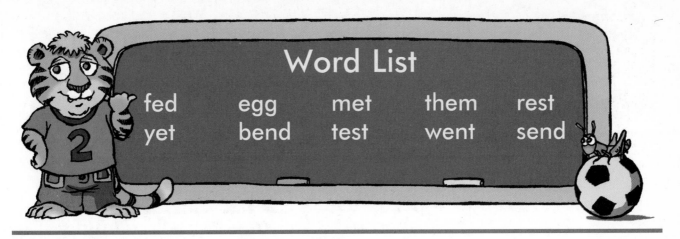

Word List

fed	egg	met	them	rest
yet	bend	test	went	send

Proofreading Practice

Here is Molly's poem. Circle the three words that are spelled wrong. Write each word correctly in the spaces below.

I mat some little blue jays,

So I gave tham all some hay.

They built a small and cozy nest.

They worked hard and did not rist!

1. _____ 2. _____ 3. _____

Review

Write a word from the word list to complete each sentence.

4. Tiger is still not here. He hasn't come _____.

5. Each chicken has an _____ in its nest.

6. Little Sister got a good grade on the spelling _____.

Spelling the Short u Sound

Eyes and Ears

Sound	Sign	Spelling
short u	/u/	mud

Word List

us

mud

rub

tug

luck

must

rug

shut

rust

stuck

Say each word. Listen for the short **u** sound in **mud.**

Study the spelling. How is the vowel sound spelled?

Write the words.
1-10. Write the ten words. Circle the letter that spells the short **u** sound.

1. _(u)s_
2. _____
3. _____
4. _____
5. _____
6. _____
7. _____
8. _____
9. _____
10. _____

Spelling Tip
The short **u** sound is often spelled **u.**

Words You Know

Complete the story with the correct words from the word list.

Car Wash

Every Saturday I _____ wash our family car. My little sister helps me. We wash off the dirt and _____. We try not to get the inside of the car wet. We always make sure to _____ the windows before we wash it. Sometimes we find some _____ on the hood. But we cannot _____ it off with a rag.

After we wash the car, we shake the sand from the _____ on the floor. Sometimes the seat gets _____. One good _____ is all it takes to move it.

With _____ we can finish the job in an hour. It makes _____ feel good when the job is done. The car looks good, too!

Word Fun: Word Meaning

Write the words from the word list that mean the same or almost the same as each word below.

1. **dirt** _____

2. **pull** _____

3. **close** _____

4. **we** _____

5. **carpet** _____

6. **scrub** _____

Words You Know

Circle the Words: Write the word in each sentence that has a word from the word list hidden in it. Then circle the word.

1. You can see a tugboat in the harbor.   _____

2. There are many rubber boots in the store.   _____

3. I will go on the bus with Bun Bun.   _____

4. They are shutting the windows.   _____

5. We are lucky to be such good friends.   _____

Break the Code: Use ABC order to fill in the missing letter in each group. Then write the word that is spelled with the underlined letters.

s <u>t</u> u   t <u>u</u> v   f <u>g</u> h   =   tug

6.   r __ t   s __ u   t __ v   b __ d   j __ l   _____

7.   q __ s   t __ v   r __ t   s __ u   _____

8.   l __ n   t __ v   c __ e   _____

9.   q __ s   t __ v   f __ h   _____

10.   l __ n   t __ v   r __ t   s __ u   _____

Rhyme and Spell: Write two words from the word list that rhyme with each word below.

duck   bug   dust

11. _____   13. _____   15. _____

12. _____   14. _____   16. _____

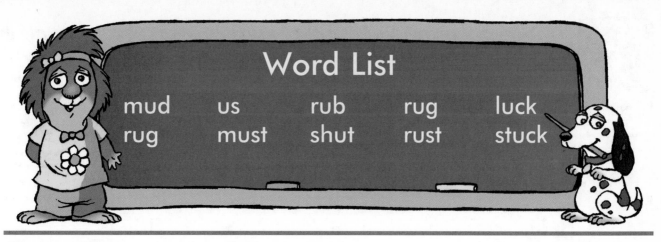

Word List

mud	us	rub	rug	luck
rug	must	shut	rust	stuck

Proofreading Practice

Here are Malcolm's directions. Circle the three words that are spelled wrong. Write each word correctly in the spaces below.

1. Shet the doors and close the windows.
2. Wash the car and rob with a rag.
3. Shake the dirt from the rog.

1. _____ 2. _____ 3. _____

Review

Write a word from the word list for each meaning below.

4. wet dirt _____

5. a cover for the floor _____

6. cannot move _____

Spelling Words with **dr**, **tr**, and **gr**

Sound	Spelling
/dr/	**dr**ive
/tr/	**tr**uck
/gr/	**gr**ade

Word List

drip

grin

tree

drum

grade

trip

drive

grand

truck

drove

Say each word. Listen for the first two sounds in **drive**, **truck**, and **grade**.

Study the spelling. How are the first two sounds spelled?

Write the words. The blends, **dr**, **tr** and **gr** are listed below. Write the words that belong under each consonant blend.

dr	**tr**	**gr**
drip	_____	_____
_____	_____	_____
_____	_____	_____
_____	_____	_____

> ## Spelling Tip
> The /dr/, /tr/, and /gr/ sounds are spelled **dr**, **tr**, and **gr**.

Words You Know

Complete the story with the correct words from the word list.

The Family Truck

Malcolm is in the second _____. His family owns a gray pickup _____. They park it in the driveway under a shady _____.

One day oil began to _____ from it. So the truck had to be taken to be fixed. It is still a _____ truck. Malcolm likes to ride in it. One day when he is older, Malcolm wants to _____ a truck just like it.

Last summer Malcolm went with his family on a _____. They _____ a long way to see some friends. Their friends gave Malcolm a present when he got there. They knew that Malcolm likes music so they gave him a big _____. Malcolm gave them a big _____ in return. He was so happy with his surprise.

Word Fun: Word Endings

Each word below has an ending. Write the word from the word list you find in each word.

1. dripped _____

2. trees _____

3. grinning _____

4. trucker _____

5. drummers _____

6. grades _____

Words You Know

Figure It Out: Write the word that is spelled after you add and subtract letters.

1.   grove - gr + dr = _____ .

2.   land - l + gr = _____ .

3.   sip - s + tr = _____ .

4.   win - w + gr = _____ .

5.   ship - sh + dr = _____ .

grove - gr + dr = ?

Think and Write: Write a word from the word list for each clue below.

6.   Someone might tell you to beat it. _____

7.   It could go from ear to ear. _____

8.   You cannot hear its bark, but you can see it. _____

9.   You need a car before you can do this. _____

10. An "A" is a good one. _____

Be an Author: Write the missing word in each book title. Use the word list to help you. Be sure to start with a capital letter.

Learn How to _____ a Car

Maps for _____ Drivers

How to Have a _____ Time

11. _____

12. _____

13. _____

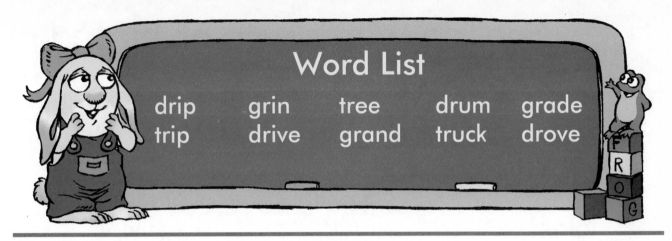

Word List

drip	grin	tree	drum	grade
trip	drive	grand	truck	drove

Proofreading Practice

Here is Little Critter's story. Circle the three words that are spelled wrong. Write each word correctly in the spaces below.

Last summer my family took a trap. we had a grond time. We drov to the lake. it was a long drive, but we had lots of fun.

1. _____ 2. _____ 3. _____

4 - 5. Two capital letters were not used at the beginning of sentences. Correct the mistakes.

Review

Write a word from the word list that fits each group of words below.

6. bark, leaf, trunk, _____

7. car, van, bus, _____

8. horn, piano, guitar, _____

Spelling Words with **gl**, **bl**, and **pl**

Eyes and Ears

Sound	Spelling
/gl/	glad
/bl/	blast
/pl/	plum

Say each word. Listen for the first two sounds in **glad**, **blast**, and **plum**.

Study the spelling. How are the first two sounds spelled?

Write the words. The blends **gl**, **bl**, and **pl** are listed below. Write the words that belong under each consonant blend.

gl	**bl**	**pl**
glad		

Word List

blast

glad

plan

blend

plus

glass

plum

blink

plot

block

Spelling Tip
The /gl/, /bl/, and /pl/ sounds
are spelled **gl**, **bl**, and **pl**.

Complete Little Sister's letter with the correct words from the word list.

Dear Grandma and Grandpa

Dear Grandma and Grandpa,

We _____ to have a picnic on the Fourth of July. I am very _____. Everyone on our _____ will come. Mom is going to make _____ pudding. We will also bring a _____ of lemonade for everyone. We will _____ fresh lemons, water, and sugar to make it.

Our town will have fireworks that night. The show will be held on a big _____ of land. We will watch the fireworks _____ off. Don't _____ or you'll miss them!

Fireworks _____ a picnic will add up to a good time for everyone. I hope you can come to our picnic.

Love,
Little Sister

Word Fun: More Than One

Add **-es** to words ending with **-s** to show more than one.
one **glass**, two **glasses**

1. one dress, two _____

2. one boss, three _____

3. one plus, four _____

4. one class, six _____

Words You Know

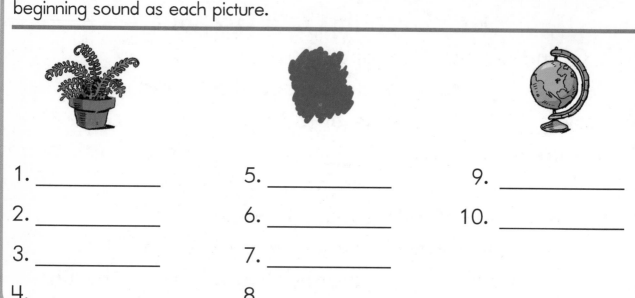

Look and Write: Write the words from the word list which have the same beginning sound as each picture.

1. _____   5. _____   9. _____

2. _____   6. _____   10. _____

3. _____   7. _____

4. _____   8. _____

Use the Dictionary: An entry word is the word you look up in a dictionary. A definition tells you what the word means. Many entry words have more than one meaning.

Look up the word **plot** in your Speller Dictionary to answer the questions.

11. **What is the entry word?** _____

12. **What is the sentence given for the first meaning?** _____

_____

13. **What is the sentence given for the second meaning?** _____

_____

14. **Which meaning is the main idea of a book?** _____

15. **Which two words come after plot?** _____ _____

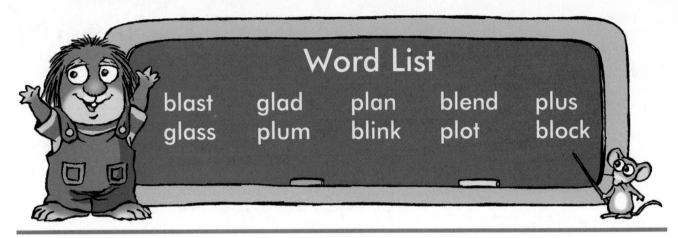

Proofreading Practice

Here is Little Sister's invitation. Circle the three words that are spelled wrong. Write each word correctly in the spaces below.

> Please plain to come to our picnic on the
> Fourth of July. I will be so glod We will have
> food plas games

1. _____ 2. _____ 3. _____

4 - 5. Two periods were not put in at the end of sentences. Correct the mistakes.

 Review

Write the sentences below. Replace the underlined word with a word from the word list.

6. Molly was <u>happy</u> that Gabby could come to the party.

_____

7. First put in the milk, then <u>mix</u> in the eggs.

_____

8. Three <u>and</u> three equals six.

_____

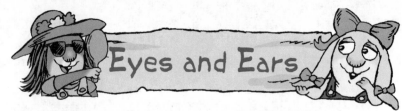

Eyes and Ears

Sound	Spelling
/sk/	ma**sk**
/mp/	ca**mp**
/ng/	wi**ng**

Word List

mask

camp

long

ask

sting

dump

wing

desk

song

jump

Say each word. Listen for the ending sounds in **mask**, **camp**, and **wing**.

Study the spelling. How are the ending sounds spelled?

Write the words. The blends **sk**, **mp**, and **ng** are listed below. Write the words that belong under each consonant blend.

sk	**mp**	**ng**
mask		

Spelling Tip

The /sk/, /mp/, and /ng/ sounds are spelled **sk**, **mp**, and **ng**.

Words You Know

Complete Little Critter's list with the correct words from the word list.

Things to Do

When you _____ in the woods, there are some things you must remember to do. Here is a list Little Critter wrote at his _____.

1. Be sure to _____ someone where you can put your tent.
2. Bugs may _____, so bring a spray.
3. Take a _____ walk every day.
4. Look for a blackbird with red feathers on its _____.
5. When you spot a raccoon, look for the _____ that seems to be on its face.
6. Watch a frog _____ over a log.
7. Sing a happy camp _____ every night.
8. Remember to _____ your trash in a can before you leave.

Word Fun: Adding -ing

Add **-ing** to the end of each word below. Write the new word.

9. camp + ing = _____

10. dump + ing = _____

11. sting + ing = _____

12. jump + ing = _____

13. ask + ing = _____

Words You Know

Finish the Rhyme: Write the word from the word list that rhymes with each underlined word.

1. Put a <u>stamp</u> on the letter to _____ .

2. Why did you toss the <u>pump</u> in the _____ ?

3. We sang a <u>song</u> that was too _____ .

4. Please <u>ask</u> them if they have a _____ .

5. When the car went over the <u>bump</u> it made me _____ .

Compare and Write: Write the missing word that finishes the sentence.

6. A fish has a fin. A bird has a _____ .

7. A rabbit can hop. A frog can _____ .

8. An artist paints a picture. A singer sings a _____ .

9. A snake can bite. A bee can _____ .

10. A teacher can write on a chalkboard.

    A student can write at a _____ .

Ask and Tell: Read each pair of sentences. Write the word **ask** if the sentence is a question. Write the word **tell** if the sentence gives an answer.

11. What is wrong with that bird? _____

12. I think it has a broken wing. _____

13. My desk is near the window. _____

14. Where is your desk in the classroom? _____

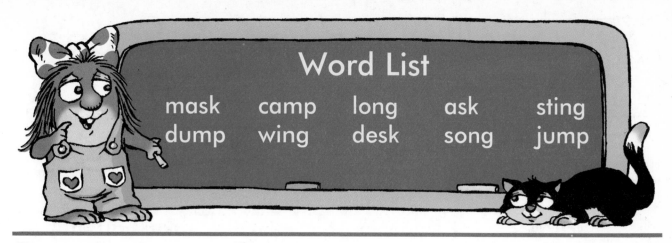

Word List

mask	camp	long	ask	sting
dump	wing	desk	song	jump

Proofreading Practice

Here are Gabby's rules. Circle the four words that are spelled wrong. Write each word correctly in the spaces below.

1.   Do not junp on the bed.

2.   Take your trash to the domp.

3.   Write a log letter home every week.

4.   Get help for a bee steng.

1. _____   2. _____   3. _____   4. _____

 Review

Write a word from the word list to finish each sentence. The missing word will rhyme with the underlined word.

5. **It rained on our tents.**

   Now we have a <u>damp</u> _____.

6. **Don't play that music.**

   That is the <u>wrong</u> _____.

7. **The bird had a <u>string</u> caught on its _____.**

Spelling the Long **a** Sound

Word List

rake

bait

say

cane

pail

hay

plate

raise

came

grape

Sound	Sign	Spelling
long a	/ā/	rake bait hay

Say each word. Listen for the long **a** sound in **rake**, **bait**, and **hay**.

Study the spelling. How is the long **a** vowel spelled in each word?

Write the words.
1-10. Write the ten words. Circle the letters that spell the long **a** sound.

1. r͟a͟k͟e͟

2. _____

3. _____

4. _____

5. _____

6. _____

7. _____

8. _____

9. _____

10. _____

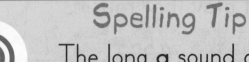

Spelling Tip
The long **a** sound can be spelled **a_e**, **ai**, and **ay**.

Words You Know

Complete the story with the correct words from the word list.

Gone Fishing

Maurice and I like to fish. We made our own fishing rods. We used an old walking _____ for one fishing rod. For the other rod, we used the handle of an old garden _____. It had been used to gather grass and _____. We used worms for _____.

Some days we have no fish to carry home in our _____. But I would _____ that we are lucky most of the time. When we _____ the fishing line out of the water, a fish is usually on the hook.

One day we _____ home with ten fish. At supper, two fresh fish were on each _____. They tasted great with some _____ juice.

Word Fun: Same Sound, Different Meaning

Circle the two words in each group with the same sound but different spellings and meanings.

1. pail, pale, peal
2. tall, tail, tale
3. hey, hi, hay

4. hole, hold, whole
5. plain, plan, plane

Words You Know

Picture This Scene: Write the six words from the word list you can find in the picture.

1. _____
2. _____
3. _____
4. _____
5. _____
6. _____

Write the Rhyme: Write the words from the word list that rhyme with each word.

7. **drape** _____

8. **bake** _____

9. **wait** _____ _____

10. **pay** _____ _____

11. **game** _____

12. **gate** _____ _____

13. **mail** _____

14. **lane** _____

Dictionary Skills: Entry words in the dictionary are in ABC order. When entry words begin with the same letter, you must look at the second letter. Write the words in each group in ABC order.

15. **plate   pole   pail**   _____ _____ _____

16. **came   crane   clay**   _____ _____ _____

17. **rust   raise   reel**   _____ _____ _____

18. **coat   cane   crab**   _____ _____ _____

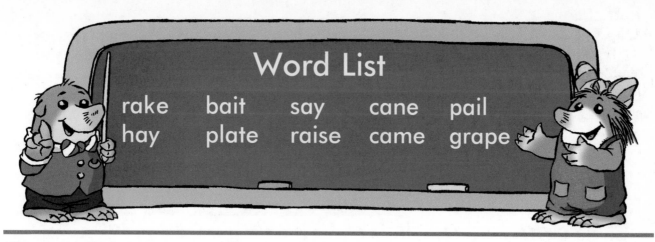

Word List

rake	bait	say	cane	pail
hay	plate	raise	came	grape

Proofreading Practice

Here is Maurice's newspaper story. Circle the four words that are spelled wrong. Write each word correctly in the spaces below.

Yesterday two big fish were caught off the town dock Worms were used for bate The fish were so big they could not fit on a dinner plat. Everyone kame to see them. Some sey they were the biggest fish they have ever seen!

1. _____ 2. _____ 3. _____ 4. _____

5 - 6. Two periods are missing at the ends of sentences. Correct the mistakes.

Review

Write a word from the word list to complete each sentence.

7. Gator used worms for _____ and caught six fish.

8. Grandma is here. Please _____ hello.

9. Little Sister piled the food on her _____.

Spelling the Long **e** Sound

Eyes and Ears

Sound	Sign	Spelling
long e	/ē/	m**ea**l s**ee**n

Word List

read

each

seen

wheel

team

deep

meal

treat

dream

sheep

Say each word. Listen for the long **e** sound in **meal** and **seen**.

Study the spelling. How is the long **e** sound spelled in each word?

Write the words.
1-10. Write the ten words. Circle the two letters that spell the long **e** sound.

1. r e a d

2. _____

3. _____

4. _____

5. _____

6. _____

7. _____

8. _____

9. _____

10. _____

Spelling Tip
The long **e** sound is spelled **ea** and **ee**.

Complete the story with the correct words from the word list.

Dreamland

Little Critter likes to _____ books. He likes make-believe stories the best. One night he fell into a _____ sleep. He had a strange _____. He dreamed about a girl and boy in one of the books.

The girl and boy had to watch over a herd of _____ all the time. They found a surprise late one day when they were about to eat their evening _____. The surprise was a real _____.

They found out that _____ bean on their dinner plates was magic! Every bean became a _____ that went around and around! On top of the wheels was a beautiful coach. It was pulled by a _____ of white horses.

The girl and boy laughed, climbed into the coach, and rode into the sky. They were never _____ again.

What a dream!

Word Fun: Same Spelling, Different Meaning

Write the word from the box that fits the two meanings below.

beat	seal	deep	meal

1. breakfast/ground corn   _____
2. animal/close an envelope   _____
3. hit again/mix together   _____
4. far down/rich in color   _____

Words You Know

Unscramble the Words: Circle the three scrambled words in the poem. Write the words correctly in the spaces below.

> Try to reda a book chae and every day,
>
> A few pages at a time will get you on your way.
>
> Many new friends you will surely meet,
>
> It will be a lot of fun and a real eattr!

1. _____   2. _____   3. _____

Write the Rhyme: Write the word from the word list that answers the question and rhymes with the underlined word.

4. What is a round hub? a <u>steel</u> _____

5. What is a very long nap? a _____ <u>sleep</u>

6. What is lunch for a sea animal? a <u>seal</u> _____

7. What is a winning sports group? a _____ <u>team</u>

Look in All Directions: Circle the six words from the word list you find hidden in the letter square.

s	v	w	x	a	d
e	t	e	a	m	e
e	e	a	c	h	e
n	s	h	e	e	p
d	r	e	a	m	w

Proofreading Practice

Here is Little Sister's book report. Circle the three words that are spelled wrong. Write each word correctly in the spaces below.

My favorite book is about shep. They live on a big farm. I red some pages ech day. It helps me learn about animals and how to treat them.

1. _____   2. _____   3. _____

✏ Review

Write a word to complete each sentence. The missing word will rhyme with the underlined word.

4. A great rest is a _____ sleep.

5. A ten-cent lunch is a deal on a _____.

6. Cold lemonade on a hot day is a _____ in the heat.

Spelling the Long i Sound

Eyes and Ears

Sound	Sign	Spelling
long i	/ī/	w**i**d**e** d**r**y n**igh**t

Word List

pine

night

cry

fight

wide

fly

light

sight

dry

right

Say each word. Listen for the long i sound in **wide**, **dry**, and **night**.

Study the spelling. How is the long i sound spelled in each word?

Write the words.
1-10. Write the ten words. Circle the letters that spell the long i sound.

1. p(i)n(e)   6. _____

2. _____   7. _____

3. _____   8. _____

4. _____   9. _____

5. _____   10. _____

Spelling Tip
The long i sound can be spelled i_e, y, and igh.

Complete the story with the correct words from the word list.

Dear Tiger

Dear Tiger,

Do you want to go for a plane ride with me? In the daytime, we will see many things because it is _____. We can _____ over houses and trees. We will soar over the long, _____ river below us. We will swoop low over a _____ forest. At _____, we will see the moon and the stars and the Critterville city lights.

We will take turns sitting near the window. That way we will not _____ over the seat. Do not get scared and _____ if the ride gets bumpy. Just _____ your eyes. Look to both the left and _____. I know you will enjoy each wonderful _____!

Your pal,
Little Critter

Word Fun: Opposites

Write the word that means the opposite of each word below.

1. day _____   4. narrow _____

2. left _____   5. laugh _____

3. wet _____   6. heavy _____

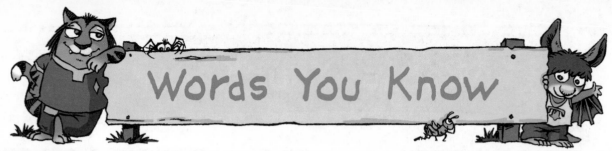

Words You Know

Look and Write: Write the words from the word list that fit each clue.

1-2. Do not _____ your kite at _____.

3-4. All _____ trucks keep to the _____.

5-6. Turn on the _____ to help your _____.

7-8. Don't _____! _____ your eyes.

9. Children should share their toys rather than _____.

Write the Words: Write the words from the word list that fit the descriptions.

Which three words end with long i spelled y?

10. _____   11. _____   12. _____

Which two words end with vowel-consonant-vowel?

13. _____   14. _____

Dictionary Skills: Many words have more than one meaning. A dictionary lists all the meanings for a word. Read the pairs of meanings. Write the word that fits both meanings.

15. an insect with two wings/move through the air _____

16. a lamp/not dark _____

17. good or correct/opposite of left _____

18. kind of tree/wish or long for something _____

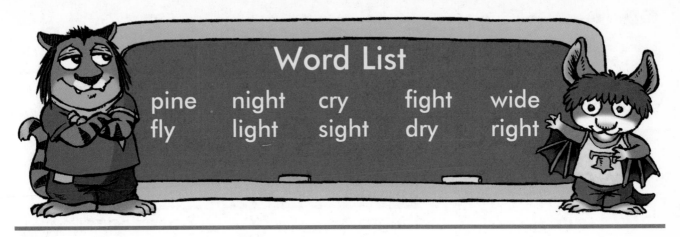

Word List

pine	night	cry	fight	wide
fly	light	sight	dry	right

Proofreading Practice

Here is Little Critter's weather report. Circle the four words that are spelled wrong. Write each word correctly in the spaces below.

today will be fair and dri. clouds will move in at
nit. It will rain rite after midnight. pilots should not
flie their planes. Stay at home until the sky clears!

1. _____   2. _____   3. _____   4. _____

5 - 7. Three sentences do not begin with capital letters.
Correct the mistakes.

✏ Review

Write a word from the word list that means the opposite of each word below.

8. wet   _____

9. wrong   _____

10. day   _____

Spelling the Long o Sound

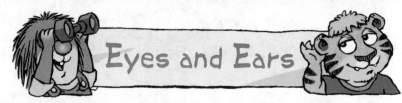
Sound	Sign	Spelling
long o	/ō/	nose coat row

Say each word. Listen for the long o sound in **nose**, **coat**, and **row**.

Study the spelling. How is the long o sound spelled in each word?

Write the words.
1-10. Write the ten words. Circle the letter that spells the long o sound.

Word List

coat

blow

nose

boat

row

those

goat

soap

snow

toad

1. c o a t

2. _____

3. _____

4. _____

5. _____

6. _____

7. _____

8. _____

9. _____

10. _____

Spelling Tip
The long o sound can be spelled o_e, oa, and ow.

Words You Know

Complete the story with the correct words from the word list.

Gabby's Report

My report is about an animal called the mountain
_____. It leaps from rock to rock like a _____ jumping
frome log to log. It races over the hills like a _____
gliding over water. It can even cling to the side of a cliff
with _____ strong hooves. It would be as hard to catch as
a wet bar of _____.

Ice and _____ often cover the rocks of its home.
Sometimes a cold wind will _____. The goat has a thick
_____ of fur to keep it warm.

The mountain goat has to
poke its _____ around to
find plants to eat. If it is lucky,
it will find a _____ of moss
on the hillside.

Word Fun: Compound Words

Add each word to a word from the word list to make a compound word.

soap+ suds = <u>soapsuds</u>   3. rain + coat = _____

1. sail + boat = _____   4. snow+ ball = _____

2. nose + dive = _____   5. toad+ stool = _____

Words You Know

Pair Them Up: Write the two missing words in each sentence. Use the picture clues to help you.

1-2. **Here is a** _____

      on a bar of _____ .

5-6. **There is a** _____

      in the _____ .

3-4. **This is a** _____

      you can _____ .

Think and Write: Write words from the word list that match each clue.

Write three words that end with a long o sound.

7. _____   8. _____   9. _____

Write two words that end with the first sound you hear in zebra.

10. _____   11. _____

Write the shortest word from the list.

12. _____

Word List

coat	blow	nose	boat	row
those	goat	soap	snow	toad

Proofreading Practice

Here is Gator's ad for a trip to the mountains. Circle the four words that are spelled wrong. Write each word correctly in the spaces below.

In summer, roe a boat or go hiking. Perhaps you will see a mountain gote or a toad. In winter, play in the snoe. Then sit by the fire when the night winds bloo.

1. _____ 2. _____ 3. _____ 4. _____

Review

Write a word from the word list for each clue below.

5. This is used in the shower. _____

6. This is what the wind does. _____

7. This is part of the face. _____

Spelling the /ü/ Sound

Eyes and Ears

Sound	Spelling
/ü/	tune moon

Word List

- tube
- zoo
- boot
- food
- tune
- pool
- soon
- rude
- moon
- room

Say each word. Listen for the /ü/ sound in **tune** and **moon**.

Study the spelling. How is the /ü/ sound spelled in each word?

Write the words.
1-10. Write the ten words. Circle the two letters that spell the vowel sound.

1. t(u)b(e)   6. _____
2. _____   7. _____
3. _____   8. _____
4. _____   9. _____
5. _____   10. _____

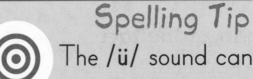

Spelling Tip
The /ü/ sound can be spelled **u_e** and **oo**.

Words You Know

Complete the story with the correct words from the word list.

Visit the Critterville Zoo

Have you ever gone to the Critterville _____ to see the animals there? You can watch the seals swim in a _____. They have a lot of _____ to swim and dive. They like to play with a ball and an old tire _____. Sometimes they will clap their flippers if someone plays them a _____.

Every day at noon, Ms. Dingo, the zoo keeper, gives them _____. Sometimes a big seal will take fish from a little seal. Do you think that is _____?

If you stay until night, you will see the _____. But you must go home _____. If not, Ms. Dingo might _____ you out!

Word Fun: Place Words

Town and room are words that name places. Circle the place word in each group.

1. pool, boot, soon

2. tune, zoo, paper

3. food, room, clock

4. house, glove, table

5. stool, park, rude

6. June, lake, tube

Words You Know

Think and Write: Write the word from the word list that is missing from each sentence.

1. **Person** is to **neighborhood** as **animal** is to _____.

2. **Head** is to **hat** as **foot** is to _____.

3. **Day** is to **sun** as **night** is to _____.

4. **Skate** is to **rink** as **swim** is to _____.

5. **Book** is to **words** as **song** is to _____.

6. **Drink** is to **water** as **eat** is to _____.

Be a News Reporter: Write the missing word that finishes each newspaper headline. Be sure to begin each word with a capital letter.

7.

Town To Get A New Swimming _____

8.

Spaceship Lands on the _____

9.

Hungry People Get _____

10.

Panda Bear Given to the _____

Use the Dictionary: Write each set of entry words in the order you find them in the dictionary.

11. rude   room   rail   _____ _____ _____

12. stem   soon   sun   _____ _____ _____

13. moon   mule   mean   _____ _____ _____

14. tube   trip   take   _____ _____ _____

15. zoo   zebra   zero   _____ _____ _____

Spelling the /ü/ Sound

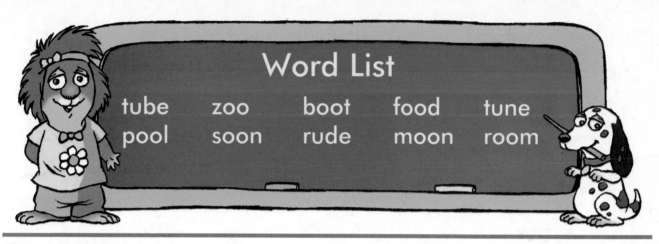

Word List

tube	zoo	boot	food	tune
pool	soon	rude	moon	room

Proofreading Practice

Here are Little Sister's questions. Circle the three words that are spelled wrong. Write each word correctly in the spaces below.

1. Do you like working at the zu?

2. What fod do you feed the lions.

3. How often do you clean the seal poole.

1. _____ 2. _____ 3. _____

4 - 5. Two question marks were not put at the ends of questions. Correct the mistakes.

Review

Write a word from the word list that fits each group of words below.

6. sun, stars, _____

7. shoe, slipper, _____

8. music, song, _____

Spelling Words with **wh** and **sh**

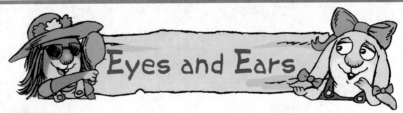

Word List

what

clash

shame

why

shine

flash

shock

where

shore

while

Sound	Spelling
/hw/ or /w/	**wh**at
/sh/	**sh**ine fla**sh**

Say each word. Listen for the first sound you hear in **what**. Listen for the first sound you hear in **shine** and the last sound you hear in **flash**. Note the signs for these sounds.

Study the spelling. How are these sounds spelled in the words?

Write the words.

1-4. Write the four words with the beginning /hw/ or /w/ sound spelled **wh**.

5-10. Write the six words with the beginning and ending /sh/ sound spelled **sh**.

1. _____what_____   5. _____

2. _____   6. _____

3. _____   7. _____

4. _____   8. _____

9. _____

10. _____

Spelling Tip

The /hw/ or /w/ sound is often spelled **wh**.

The /sh/ sound is often spelled **sh**.

Words You Know

Complete the story with the correct words from the word list.

The Critterville School Band

Can you guess the reason _____ Little Critter plays in the Critterville School Band? He loves to hear the _____ of the cymbals.

The places _____ the band plays are always different. Once, they played as they marched along the _____ of a lake. They had lots of fun.

At first, the day was nice. Little Critter hoped the sun would _____ all day. Suddenly, it started to grow darker and darker. Then the band members saw a _____ of light! Soon after, they heard claps of thunder.

The storm came as a _____ to everyone. The band members were all wet. "_____ a _____!" said the band leader.

Word Fun: Compound Words

Add a word from the word list to each word below. Write the compound

mean + while = <u>meanwhile</u>

1. _____ + light = _____

2. some + _____ = _____

3. sun + _____ = _____

4. _____ + ever = _____

5. _____ + line = _____

Words You Know

Find a Rhyme: Write the word from the word list that rhymes with the underlined word or part of a word in each sentence.

1. Can you <u>smile</u> for a little _____?

2. I feel <u>fine</u> when the sun does _____.

3. Is there a book<u>store</u> near the sea_____?

4. When I fell off the <u>rock</u>, it was a big _____.

Look and Spell: Write the words from the word list that answer the questions.

Which four words have the same beginning sound as 👞 ?

5. _____   6. _____   7. _____   8. _____

Which two words have the same ending sound as 🐟 ?

9. _____   10. _____

Which four words have the same beginning sound as ⊕ ?

11. _____   12. _____   13. _____   14. _____

Write the Questions: Write a question to go with each answer. Be sure to use **what, where,** or **why** in your question. Remember to end each question with a question mark. Circle each question word that you use.

15. **Question:** _____
    Answer: They are at the shore.

16. **Question:** _____
    Answer: We are looking for seashells.

17. **Question:** _____
    Answer: We need the shells for the science fair.

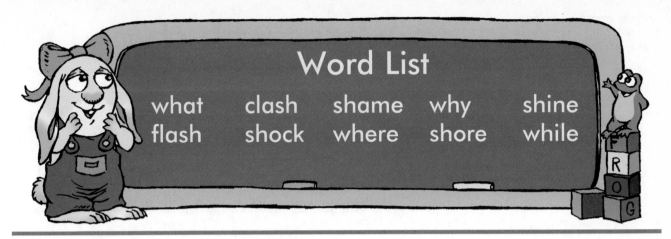

Proofreading Practice

Here are the words to a song that Molly wrote. Circle the three words that are spelled wrong. Write each word correctly in the spaces below.

Oh, wy did you move?

Oh, wher are you now?

It is such a sham,

Nothing is the same without you.

1. _____ 2. _____ 3. _____

✏ Review

Write a word from the word list for each clue below.

4. a question word that rhymes with <u>air</u> _____

5. a bright light that rhymes with <u>dash</u> _____

6. land that is next to a lake or sea that rhymes with <u>more</u>

_____

Spelling Words with **ch** and **th**

Eyes and Ears

Sound	Spelling
/ch/	choke
/th/	thank with

Word List

much

thing

such

choke

tooth

thank

bath

thin

teach

with

Say each word. Listen for the first sound you hear in **choke** and **thank**. Listen for the last sound you hear in **with**. Note the signs for these sounds.

Study the spelling. How are the /**ch**/ and /**th**/ sounds spelled in the words?

Write the words.
1-4. Write the four words spelled with the beginning and ending /**ch**/ sound.
5-10. Write the six words spelled with the beginning and ending /**th**/ sound.

1. ___much___
2. _____
3. _____
4. _____

5. _____
6. _____
7. _____
8. _____
9. _____
10. _____

Spelling Tip

The /**ch**/ and /**th**/ sounds are spelled **ch** and **th**.

Words You Know

Complete the story with the correct words from the word list.

Growing Up

On Saturday I woke up _____ all my teeth in my mouth. But the _____ that would change that was an apple.

I had so _____ to do that day. First, I wanted to _____ my dog, Blue, a new trick. While we were playing, Blue ran into a big mud puddle. So I had to give him a _____. Blue did not _____ me after I was done!

Then I stopped for lunch. After eating my sandwich, I ate an apple. I try to eat every meal so I will not be too _____!

All of a sudden, my _____ fell out when I bit into the apple. It was _____ a surprise! I was lucky that I did not swallow my tooth and _____. I hope my new tooth will grow in soon!

Word Fun: Word Endings

Add **-er** to the end of each word to show **a person who.**

buy + er = buyer

1. teach + er = _____

2. paint + er = _____

3. climb + er = _____

4. catch + er = _____

5. speak + er _____

Words You Know

Finish the Puzzles: Fill in the words from the word list that fit each puzzle.

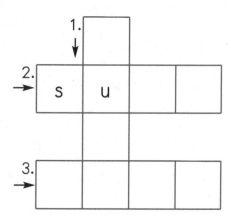

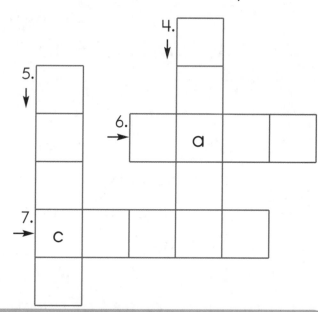

Hide and Seek: Write the words from the word list hidden in each ad.

8. _____

Buy two
toothbrushes.
Get one free.

9. _____

THIS WEEK ONLY
All bathtubs
on sale!

10. _____

A treat without
a fuss!
Try new Snack Bars.

Use the Dictionary: A dictionary entry often gives a sample sentence to help explain a word's meaning. Look up the words below in the Speller Dictionary in the back of this book. Then write your own sentence for each of these words.

11. **teach** _____

12. **thank** _____

13. **bath** _____

14. **thing** _____

Spelling Words with **ch** and **th**

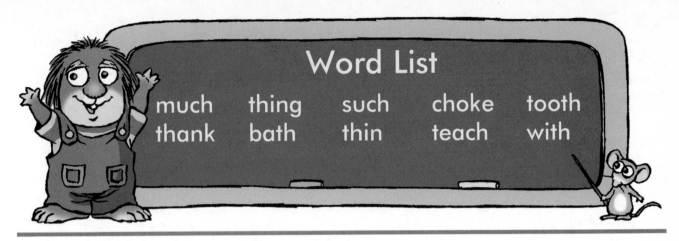

Word List

much	thing	such	choke	tooth
thank	bath	thin	teach	with

Proofreading Practice

Here is one of Malcolm's diary entries. Circle the four words that are spelled wrong. Write each word correctly in the spaces below.

> today I lost my front tuth. I was taking a bathe
> and playing whith my toys. suddenly it fell out. It
> was a strange thig to happen.

1. _____ 2. _____ 3. _____ 4. _____

5 - 6. Two capital letters were not put at the beginning of sentences. Correct the mistakes.

 # Review

Write a word from the word list to fill in the blank in each pair of sentences. The missing word will rhyme with the underlined word.

7. Gator adds numbers when he is in the tub.
   Gator likes to do <u>math</u> in the _____.

8. A thick rug is a fat mat.
   A skinny needle is a _____ <u>pin</u>.

9. Miss Kitty holds classes on the shore.
   She likes to _____ at the <u>beach</u>.

Spelling the **Vowel + r** Sound

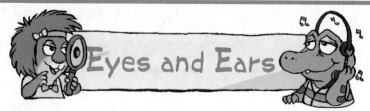

Eyes and Ears

Sound	Spelling
/är/	c**ar**t

Word List

farm

cart

dark

yard

art

barn

park

start

hard

sharp

Say each word. Listen for the **vowel + r** sound you hear in **cart**. Note the sign for this sound.

Study the spelling. How is the /**är**/ sound spelled in each word?

Write the words.

1-10. Write the ten words. Circle the letters that spell the /**är**/ sound.

1. f **ar** m

2. _____

3. _____

4. _____

5. _____

6. _____

7. _____

8. _____

9. _____

10. _____

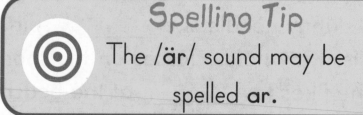

Spelling Tip
The /**är**/ sound may be spelled **ar**.

Complete the story with the correct words from the word list.

Down on the Farm

My Grandma and Grandpa live on a small _____.
Like most farmers, they work very _____. They have to
_____ their chores early. Just after sunrise, they fill a
_____ with feed for the pigs. Then they head for the
_____ to milk the cows. Sometimes they work until it is
_____.

On the weekends there are chores to do around the
house. They have to cut the grass in the front _____. Of
course, if the blades on the mower are _____, the work
goes faster.

Then they have time for some fun. Sometimes they like
to go to the baseball _____ to watch the home team
play. Other times they take painting lessons at the _____
school. They always like to keep busy.

Word Fun: Comparing Things

The endings -er and -est are used to compare. -Er is used to compare two
things. -Est is used to compare 3 or more things. Add -er and -est to each word.

hard   harder   hardest   3. dark _____ _____

1. sharp _____ _____   4. long _____ _____

2. short _____ _____   5. smart _____ _____

Words You Know

Find and Change: Write the word from the word list that means the opposite of the underlined word.

1. It is <u>easy</u> to learn to roller skate. _____

2. I painted the sky <u>light</u> blue in the picture. _____

3. The blade on the knife is <u>dull</u>. _____

4. When will the bus <u>stop</u>? _____

Answer the Riddle: Write the words from the word list that answer the riddles.

5. I am a building. I am red. Horses and cows live in me. _____

6. I am outside of a house or school.
   Sometimes children play on my grass. _____

7. I have wheels. I carry things. _____

8. I am land. People grow all kinds of crops on me. _____

9. I am a big open space where people like to picnic.
   I have grass and trees. Sometimes I am in the city. _____

Finish the Book Cover: Write titles for the books using the following words: **art, farm, park.** Be sure to begin words in your book titles with capital letters.

10. _____

11. _____

12. _____

_____   _____   _____

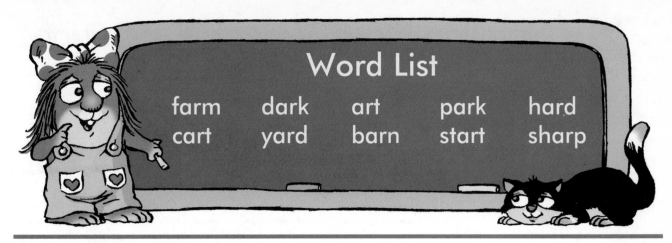

Word List

farm	dark	art	park	hard
cart	yard	barn	start	sharp

Proofreading Practice

Here is Grandpa's list of chores. Circle the three words that are spelled wrong. Write each word correctly in the spaces below.

Farm Chores

1. Clean the born.
2. Fill the carte with hay.
3. Rake the yerd.
4. Feed the cows.

1. _____   2. _____   3. _____

Review

Write a word from the word list that fits each group of words.

4. night, black, shadow, _____

5. pin, knife, ouch, _____

6. trees, swings, slides, _____

Spelling More **Vowel + r** Sounds

Eyes and Ears

Word List

girl

more

bird

horse

dirt

horn

short

first

for

shirt

Sound	Spelling	
/ûr/	bird	girl
/ôr/	horn	for

Say each word. Listen for the **vowel + r** sound in **bird** and **girl**. Listen for the **vowel + r** sound in **horn** and **for**. Note the signs for these sounds.

Study the spelling. How are the /**ûr**/ and /**ôr**/ sounds spelled in each word?

Write the words.
1-5. Write the five words spelled with the /ûr/ sound.
6-10. Write the five words spelled with the /ôr/ sound.

1. ____girl____   6. _____
2. _____   7. _____
3. _____   8. _____
4. _____   9. _____
5. _____   10. _____

Spelling Tip

The /**ûr**/ sound may be spelled **ir**.
The /**ôr**/ sound may be spelled **or**.

Complete the story with the correct words from the word list.

Early One Morning

Bun Bun woke up very early one morning when she heard a car _____. Nobody in the house was awake yet.

The young _____ got out of bed quickly. She put on a pair of pants and a _____. She wanted to enjoy her _____ day of summer vacation.

Bun Bun went outside after she fixed herself some breakfast. A small brown _____ greeted her with a song. She headed _____ the barn. It was only a _____ walk away.

Inside the barn, her _____ was waiting in a stall. He dug his hoof in the _____ when he saw her. Bun Bun fed him some hay. She would give him some _____ to eat later. Then she went riding.

Word Fun: Number Words

Number words tell **how many** and **which order**. Write the number word for each critter's place in line.   third   first   fifth   second   fourth

_____   _____   _____   _____   _____

Words You Know

Be a Magician: Take away one word from the letters in each box. Write the word that is left.

1. Take away . Find a farm animal.

horhayse

_____

2. Take away . Find something in a band.

honotern

_____

3. Take away . Find something to wear.

shiballrt

_____

4. Take away . Find something to dig in.

dipailrt

_____

5. Take away . Find a person.

gimaskrl

_____

Fill It In: Write the missing word. Be sure to begin each word with a capital letter.

6.
_____
Sale

7.
_____
Prize

8.
Save
_____
Here!

9.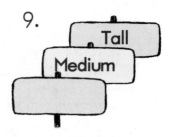
Tall
Medium
_____

Use the Dictionary: Many words have more than one meaning. Look up the word **horn** in the Speller Dictionary in the back of this book. Write two sentences using **horn**. Each sentence must use a different meaning for **horn**.

10. _____

11. _____

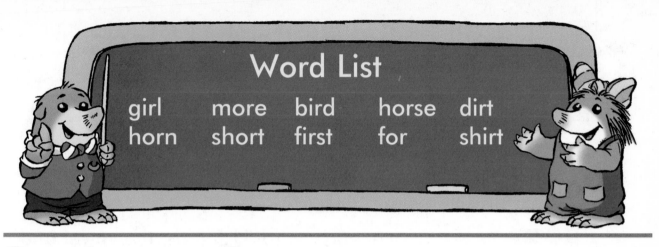

Word List

girl   more   bird   horse   dirt
horn   short   first   for   shirt

Proofreading Practice

Here is Bat Child's plan. Circle the five words that are spelled wrong. Write each word correctly in the spaces below.

8:00-9:00	Make breakfast fer my family.
9:00-10:00	Buy a new red shert.
10:00-11:00	Go for a ride on my hors.
11:00-12:00	Repair the berd cage one mor time.

1. _____ 3. _____ 5. _____

2. _____ 4. _____

Review

Write a word from the word list that means the opposite of each word below.

6. boy   _____

7. last   _____

8. tall   _____

Easily Misspelled Words

Eyes and Ears

Word List

does
gone
who
any
your
give
very
were
live
every

Say each word. Listen for the vowel and consonant sounds.

Study the spelling. Look for unusual or tricky spellings.

Write the words.
1-10. Write the ten words. Circle any spellings you find unusual. Try to remember them.

1. _____does_____   6. _____
2. _____   7. _____
3. _____   8. _____
4. _____   9. _____
5. _____   10. _____

Spelling Tip
Some words do not follow common spelling patterns.

Complete the story with the correct words from the word list.

Road Race

Is there someone you know _____ likes to run? Maybe it is a friend or someone in _____ family. Maybe it is you! These days there are many people who are runners.

Running is a good way to keep fit. It _____ not matter if you _____ in the city or in the country. You can find a place to run _____ day.

Some day you might like to enter a race. Are there _____ races near where you live? Have you ever even _____ to a race? Some races are _____ long. Each runner has to go over 26 miles to reach the finish line. The runners have to _____ their best. How do you think you would feel if you _____ in such a long race?

Word Fun: Same Spelling, Different Word

Write a word from the box that fits both blanks in each sentence.

live	does	close	wind

1. _____ a door _____ to you.   3. _____ the baby see the _____?

2. I _____ near a _____ lion.   4. _____ a rope in the _____.

Words You Know

Add the Vowels: Fill in the missing vowels. Then write the words that are spelled. Be sure to remember that the letter **y** is sometimes used as a vowel. Use the word list to help you.

1. g __ n __   _____
2. __ n __   _____
3. w __ r __   _____
4. g __ v __   _____
5. d __ __ s   _____

6. __ v __ r __   _____
7. l __ v __   _____
8. y __ __ r   _____
9. wh __   _____
10. v __ r __   _____

Answer and Write: Write the words from the word list that answer the questions.

11. Which word is a question word? _____

12. Which word has the word **very** in it? _____

13-15. Which three words end with a long **e** sound that is spelled **y**?

_____   _____   _____

Find the Meaning: Write the words that can be used in place of the underlined words in each sentence.

16. Teachers <u>hand over</u> books to their students. _____

17. I hope to read a book <u>each</u> week. _____

18. The child is <u>so</u> happy with the bike. _____

19. Would you like <u>some</u> grapes to eat? _____

20. The painter has <u>moved</u> from the city. _____

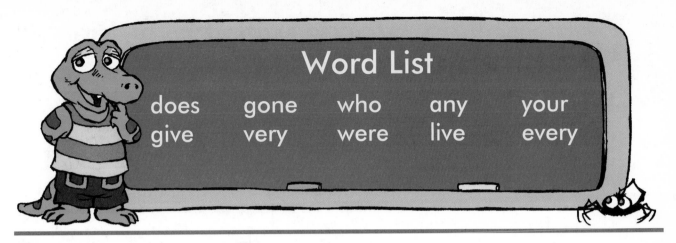

Word List

does   gone   who   any   your

give   very   were   live   every

Proofreading Practice

Here is Little Critter's postcard. Circle the four words that are spelled wrong. Write each word correctly in the spaces below.

> Dear Tiger,
>
> I am vary happy you won the race. Did they giv you a medal Will you run in eny more races Wu came in second?
>
> Your pal,
>
> Little Critter

1. _____ 2. _____ 3. _____ 4. _____

5 - 6. Two question marks were not put at the ends of questions. Correct the mistakes.

Review

Write a word from the word list to fill the blank in each pair of sentences.

7. **Little Sister: Did you eat all the carrots?**

   Bun Bun: Yes, I ate _____ one of them.

8. **Gator: Is this my jacket?**

   Tiger: Yes, it is _____ jacket.

9. **Maurice: Did you like the popcorn?**

   Molly: Yes, it was _____ good!

Spelling Words with **br**, **fr**, and **tr**

Word List

- train
- brag
- free
- trade
- frog
- brick
- frisky
- bright
- trick
- broom

Sound	Spelling
/br/	**br**ick
/fr/	**fr**og
/tr/	**tr**ade

Say each word. Listen for the first two sounds in **brick**, **frog**, and **trade**.

Study the spelling. How are the two beginning sounds spelled?

Write the words. The blends **br**, **fr** and **tr** are listed below. Write the words that belong under each consonant blend.

br	**fr**	**tr**
brag	_____	_____
_____	_____	_____
_____	_____	_____
_____	_____	_____

Spelling Tip

The /br/, /fr/, and /tr/ sounds are spelled **br**, **fr**, and **tr**.

Words You Know

Complete the story with the correct words from the word list.

My Pet Frog and I

I have a new pet _____. I found it in a pond. So I got it for _____!

I try not to _____ too much about my pet. It is a great frog. My frog is a _____ green color. My frog is also very smart and very _____. I plan to _____ my frog to do tricks. One _____ it has already learned is to jump through a hoop that I am holding.

My friend, Little Critter, also has a pet frog. Sometimes we race our frogs on the red _____ path in front of my house. We use the handle of a _____ for the finish line.

Sometimes my frog wins. Sometimes Little Critter's frog comes in first. Either way, I would not _____ my frog for anything. No, not ever!

Word Fun: Many Meanings

Some words have more than one meaning. Write the word from the word list that has both meanings.

1. railroad cars; to teach _____

2. shiny; smart _____

3. no cost; to set loose _____

4. swap; job to make money _____

5. fool or cheat; a clever act _____

Words You Know

Join the Pieces: Write the five words from the word list that are spelled by putting the bricks together. Be sure to use each brick part only one time.

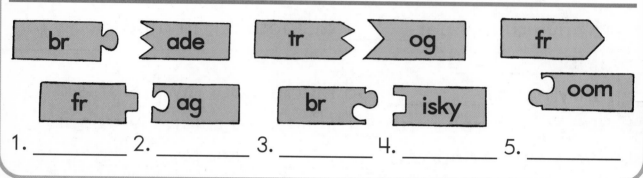

br   ade   tr   og   fr

fr   ag   br   isky   oom

1. _____   2. _____   3. _____   4. _____   5. _____

Spell the Words: Write the words from the word list that fit the clues.

Two words that rhyme with sick.

6. _____   7. _____

Two words that have double vowels.

8. _____   9. _____

The word that ends with long e spelled y.

10. _____

The word that rhymes with fright.

11. _____

Put on Your Thinking Cap: Write the word that finishes each sentence.

12. You scrub with a mop. You sweep with a _____.

13. A bus travels on a road. A _____ travels on a track.

14. A fish can swim. A _____ can hop.

15. Some houses are made of wood.

     Some houses are made of _____.

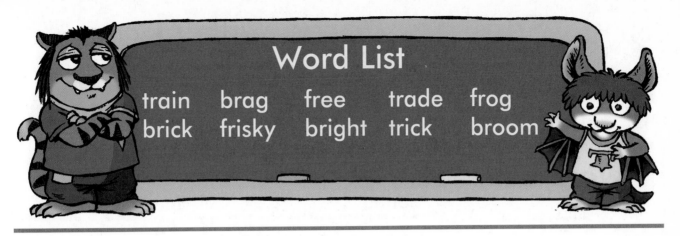

Word List

train   brag   free   trade   frog
brick   frisky   bright   trick   broom

Proofreading Practice

Here is Tiger's story. Circle the three words that are spelled wrong. Write each word correctly in the spaces below.

> I have a new pet frog. It is brite green. I found it when I went fishing last week It is very friske. It would be fun to train it to do some trecks

1. _____   2. _____   3. _____

4 - 5. Two periods were not put in at the ends of sentences. Correct the mistakes.

✏ Review

Write a word from the word list that fits each group of words.

6. mop, sweep, dust, _____

7. snake, toad, pond, _____

8. airplane, bus, tracks, _____

Spelling Words with **sl** and **sp**

Eyes and Ears

Word List

slam

spin

speed

slip

space

slide

slick

speech

spy

sled

Sound	Spelling
/sl/	**sl**ip
/sp/	**sp**in

Say each word. Listen for the first two sounds in **slip** and **spin**.

Study the spelling. How are the first two sounds spelled?

Write the words.
1-5. Write the five words that begin with **sl**.
6-10. Write the five words that begin with **sp**.

1. _____slam_____   6. _____
2. _____   7. _____
3. _____   8. _____
4. _____   9. _____
5. _____   10. _____

Spelling Tip
The /**sl**/ and /**sp**/ sounds
are spelled **sl** and **sp**.

Words You Know

Complete the story with the correct words from the word list.

Fun in the Winter

I love the winter. There is so much to do. When it snows, I pull my _____ to the top of a hill. Then I get on and _____ down. I pick up _____ going down. It feels as if I am flying through _____.

But I must watch where I am going. At the first sign of snow, our teacher, Miss Kitty, gives the class a _____ on safety. We have to be careful so we do not _____ into a tree.

If there is no snow, I go ice skating. I like to skate on ice that is smooth and _____. Sometimes I _____ and fall. I hope no one is watching! Other times I _____ like a top! Then I hope my friends will _____ on me to see how well I skate!

Word Fun: Action Words

Slam and **spin** describe things that you can do. Circle the action word in each pair of words.

1. talk, book
2. van, drive
3. smile, story
4. apple, eat
5. sleep, cot
6. food, share

Words You Know

Seek and Find: Circle the five words from the word list hidden in the letter square. Be sure to look both across and down. Write the words in the blanks below.

c	a	s	p	i	n	t
d	e	l	o	s	p	y
s	l	i	d	e	k	m
r	s	p	e	e	c	h

1. _____
2. _____
3. _____
4. _____
5. _____

Give a Speech: Write the missing word in each title. Be sure you begin each word in the title with a capital letter.

6. How to _____ a Top

7. Two ways to _____ Downhill with a Sled

8. Don't _____! You'll Get There.

9. My Life as a _____

Finish the Sign: Write the missing word in each sign.

| Do not _____ the door! | 55 mph _____ Limit | Slow. Road _____ When Wet. | For Sale: Ice Skates and _____ | _____ Center Next Exit |

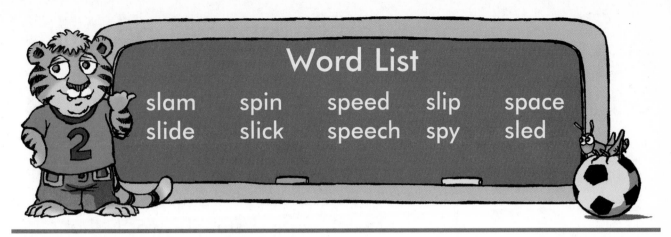

Word List

slam	spin	speed	slip	space
slide	slick	speech	spy	sled

Proofreading Practice

Here is Little Sister's poem. Circle the three words that are spelled wrong. Write each word correctly in the spaces below.

Ice Skating

I slep and slied,

I just cannot glide.

Please give me more spase,

So I do not fall on my face!

1. _____ 2. _____ 3. _____

Review

Write a word from the word list for each clue below.

4. something for riding on snow _____

5. turn around _____

6. to watch secretly _____

Spelling Words that Sound Alike

Eyes and Ears

Word List

see

sea

dear

deer

meet

meat

road

rode

dye

die

Say each word. Listen for words that sound alike.

Study the spelling. How are the words spelled? Do some words have the same sounds but different spellings and meanings?

Write the words.
1-10. Write a word. Then write a word that sounds the same. Write all ten words.

1. ___see___   6. _____

2. _____   7. _____

3. _____   8. _____

4. _____   9. _____

5. _____   10. _____

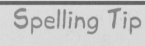

Spelling Tip

Some words have the same sounds but different spellings and meanings.

Words You Know

Complete the story with the correct words from the word list.

A Trip to the Sea

Last summer I went on a trip with my grandma and grandpa. We _____ in their new car. We could _____ many things along the way. We saw a little _____ running along the _____. It ran right in front of our car. Luckily, we did not hit it. I was glad it did not get hurt and _____.

Later, we stopped by the _____ to watch the surfers and the sailboats. Then, we got some grape popsicles. Mine melted all over my shirt. Grandma said I looked like I had purple _____ all over me!

That night, Mom and Dad wanted to _____ us for dinner. I hoped we would have pizza, but Grandpa wanted _____ and potatoes. At dinner, I told Mom and Dad about our trip.

Mom hugged me. "I'm glad you had such a nice day, _____," she said.

Word Fun: Abbreviations

Rd. is an abbreviation for **Road.** Match the correct abbreviation with each word.

Doctor	St.
Mister	Dr.
Street	Mr.
Avenue	Nov.
November	Ave.

Words You Know

Look and Write: Write the words from the word list that fit each clue.

1. look at _____
2. an ocean _____
3. you drive on it _____
4. went by bus _____
5. someone loved _____
6. an animal _____
7. something to eat _____
8. come together _____
9. stop living _____
10. used to color _____

Puzzle Play: Fill in the pair of words from the word list that fits in each puzzle. Be sure they rhyme with the word beside the puzzle.

11.

toad

r

12.

here

e

d | | | r

13.

feet

m

e | t

14.

bee

e

a

15.

fly

y | e

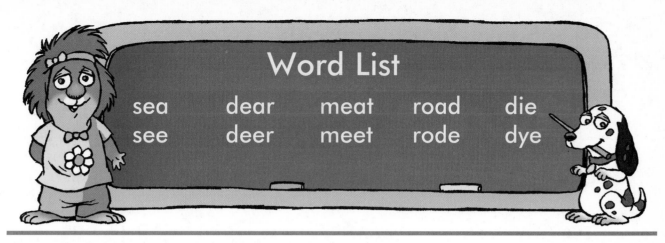

Word List

| sea | dear | meat | road | die |
| see | deer | meet | rode | dye |

Proofreading Practice

Here is Little Critter's letter. Circle the four words that are spelled wrong. Write each word correctly in the spaces below.

> Dear Gator,
>
> I went to visit my friend Zack. I drove on a bumpy rode. We saw a dear. I had a great time. It was a real treat to meat his family. I hope I will sea them again soon.
>
> Your friend,
> Little Critter

1. _____ 2. _____ 3. _____ 4. _____

Review

Write a word from the word list to fill the blank in each pair of sentences.

5. **Little Critter: Look at that red bird!**
   Dad: I can't _____ it anywhere.

6. **Little Sister: That dress is an ugly color.**
   Mom: Why don't we _____ it a new color?

7. **Maurice: Why is Mom's car still here?**
   Molly: She _____ her bike to work today.

Spelling Family Names

Eyes and Ears

Word List

family

mother

sister

grandmother

aunt

baby

grandfather

uncle

father

brother

Say each word. Listen for vowel and consonant sounds you know.

Study the spelling. Look for spellings you know.

Write the words.
1-6. Write the six words that end with **er**.
7-8. Write the two words that end with long **e** spelled **y**.
9-10. Write **aunt** and **uncle**. Circle the vowels in each word.

1. _____   6. _____

2. _____   7. _____

3. _____   8. _____

4. _____   9. _____

5. _____   10. _____

Words You Know

Complete the story with the correct words from the word list.

My Family

My name is Maurice. I have a large _____. I have a twin _____ named Molly. I call my _____ Mom, and I call my _____ Dad. Someday, I hope my mother has another _____. I want a little _____!

My mother's sister is my _____. My mother's mother is my _____. I like when they come to Critterville to visit. They always tell funny stories about Mom.

My father's brother is my _____. My father's father is my _____. They take Molly and me fishing every summer. I love my family!

Word Fun: Pronouns

Write each sentence using **He**, **She**, **They**, or **We** in place of the underlined words.

1. <u>My mother</u> will sing. _____

2. <u>You and I</u> can go. _____

3. <u>Our sister and brother</u> ski. _____

4. <u>His uncle</u> works at home. _____

5. <u>Her grandmother</u> has a cat. _____

Words You Know

Map the Family: Fill in the missing letters. Then write the words that are spelled.

7. _ _ _ _ _ mother   8. _ _ _ _ _ father

_____   _____

5. _ _ nt   3. m _ ther   4. f _ ther   6. _ _ cle

_____   _____   _____   _____

1. sis _ _ _   2. bro _ _ _ _

_____   _____

Meet the Family: Write the words from the word list that fit each clue.

9. mom's sister _____   13. **boy child** _____

10. **dad's brother** _____   14. girl child _____

11. dad's mother _____   15. all of the people _____

12. mom's father _____   16. very young child _____

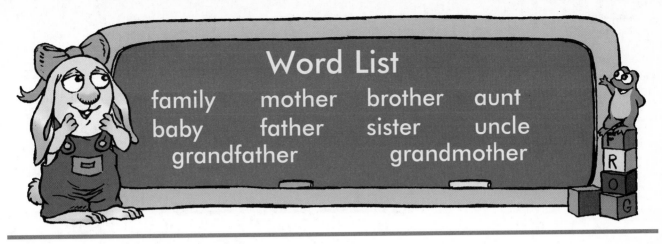

Word List

family	mother	brother	aunt
baby	father	sister	uncle
grandfather		grandmother	

Proofreading Practice

Here is Bun Bun's description of a family member. Circle the four words that are spelled wrong. Write each word correctly in the spaces below.

Why is my ant so special. She is the one in my famly who can do everything. She can fix a car. She is a great cook. She tells funny stories to my broter and sistre.

1. _____ 2. _____ 3. _____ 4. _____

5. One question mark was not put at the end of a question. Correct the mistake.

 ## Review

Write a word from the word list that goes with each word below as in the example. grandmother - grandfather

6. mother – _____

7. sister – _____

8. aunt – _____

Spelling the / u̇/ Sound

Eyes and Ears

Sound	Spelling
/u̇/	push hook

Say each word. Listen for the vowel sound you hear in **push** and **hook**. Note the sign for this sound.

Study the spelling. How is the vowel sound spelled in each word?

Write the words.
1-10. Write the ten words. Circle the letter that spells the /u̇/ sound.

Word List

put

hook

full

took

push

foot

book

pull

look

good

1. p(u)t

2. _____

3. _____

4. _____

5. _____

6. _____

7. _____

8. _____

9. _____

10. _____

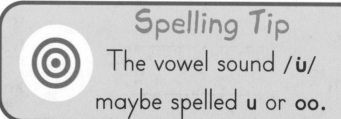

Spelling Tip
The vowel sound /u̇/ maybe spelled **u** or **oo**.

Words You Know

Complete the story with the correct words from the word list.

Another Fish Story

Malcolm wanted to learn how to fish. So he went to the library to _____ for a _____. The shelves were _____ of all kinds of books. He soon found a guide to fishing that looked as if it would be _____. He _____ it out.

The book told Malcolm everything he ever wanted to know about fishing. He even learned how to tie the _____ to the fishing line.

One day, Malcolm got into a rowboat for the first time. He did not even know where to _____ each _____. He started to _____ the oars toward him and then _____ them away. But the boat did not move. Malcolm

Word Fun: More Than One

Write the plurals of the underlined words below. Use the words in the word box.

men	feet	children	mice

1. one <u>foot</u>, two _____   3. one <u>child</u>, two _____

2. one <u>man</u>, two _____   4. one <u>mouse</u>, two _____

Words You Know

Dial a Word: Turn the letters on the dial to write four words.

1. _____
2. _____
3. _____
4. _____

l + c b ook

Change the Meaning: Write the words that are the opposites of the underlined words.

5. The apple tasted <u>bad</u>.
   _____

6. Who <u>gave</u> these books?
   _____

7. My glass is <u>empty</u>.
   _____

8. Will you <u>push</u> the cart?
   _____

Write a Rhyme: Write the words that finish the rhymes.

9. "After I fix supper," said the cook.
   "I will read a good _____."

10. I sat for a while by the brook.
    Then I put some bait on my _____.

11. I know for sure that is the crook!
    I got a very close _____.

12. It is a shopping cart, not a rose bush.
    Please help me and give it a _____.

13. I need a place for my left foot.
    Where do you think it can be _____?

14. The chimney was full of soot.
    When I tried to clean it, soot dropped on my _____.

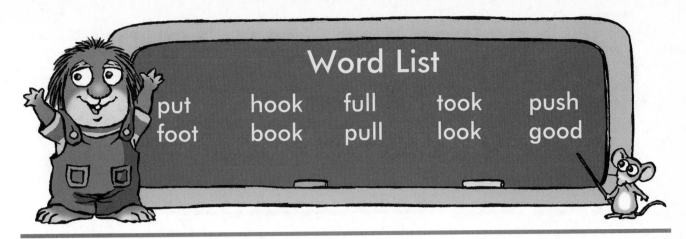

Word List

put	hook	full	took	push
foot	book	pull	look	good

Proofreading Practice

Here is Gabby's book report. Circle the three words that are spelled wrong. Write each word correctly in the spaces below.

> **Amelia Bedelia** is a funny buk. Amelia is a gud cook, but she gets things mixed up. She poot bows on a chicken. She took some lightbulbs outside and hung them on a clothesline. I would like her as a friend!

1. _____ 2. _____ 3. _____

Review

Write a word from the word list to finish each sentence. The missing word will rhyme with the underlined word.

4. A nice log is _____ __wood__.

5. To press on a little tree is to _____ a __bush__.

6. At the library you __look__ for a _____.

Spelling the /ou/ Sound

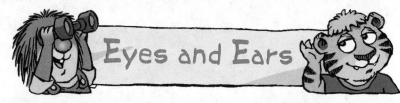

Word List

out

now

clown

our

down

sound

owl

house

town

loud

Eyes and Ears

Sound	Spelling
/ou/	town sound

Say each word. Listen for the vowel sound in **town** and **sound**.

Study the spelling. How is the /**ou**/ sound spelled in each word?

Write the words.

1-10. Write the ten words. Circle the letters that spell the /**ou**/ sound.

1. ___(ou)t___   6. _____

2. _____   7. _____

3. _____   8. _____

4. _____   9. _____

5. _____   10. _____

Spelling Tip

The /**ou**/ sound may be spelled **ow** and **ou**.

Complete the story with the correct words from the word list.

The Circus

Listen, everybody! The circus has come to _____. You do not have to leave your _____ to buy tickets for the show. Call right _____. Bring the whole family.

You will laugh at a funny _____ riding on a horse. You will see two acrobats shot _____ of a cannon. Then they will come _____ in a net. Just remember to block your ears. The _____ of the cannon blast is very _____! You will see _____ amazing skywalkers cross the wire.

You can come to the circus during the day. Or, you can come in the evening if you are a night _____. Do not delay! Call today!

Word Fun: Words That Tell When

Now tells when something is happening. Circle the word in each pair that tells when.

1. today, town
2. newspaper, never
3. always, apple

4. sometimes, sun
5. talk, tomorrow
6. yesterday, yawn

Words You Know

Look and Write: Write the words from the word list that have the same ending sounds as the picture names.

1. _____   3. _____   5. _____   7. _____

2. _____   4. _____   6. _____   8. _____

9. _____

10. _____

Rhyme and Write: Finish the sentences with words that rhyme with the underlined words.

11. A person who is sad in the circus is a <u>frown</u> _____.

12. A bird on something you dry with is an _____ <u>towel</u>.

13. A little creature in your home is a _____ <u>mouse</u>.

Finish the News: Write the missing word from the word list that finishes the newspaper headline. Be sure to begin each word with a capital letter.

14.
The Circus is Coming to
_____

15.
_____
Rocket Blasts Off!

16.
Car Runs
_____
of Gas on Highway

Word List

sound	now	clown	our	down
out	owl	house	town	loud

Proofreading Practice

Here is Little Sister's list. Circle the three words that are spelled wrong. Write each word correctly in the spaces below.

Ways to Make Your Friends Laugh

1. Make a funny sownd.

2. Say up when you mean down.

3. Dress up like a cloun.

4. Hoot like an oul.

5. Draw a silly picture of your brother.

1. _____ 2. _____ 3. _____

✏ Review

Write a word from the word list that means the same as each underlined part of the poems below.

4. "This is the <u>home</u> that Jack built." _____
   — Nursery Rhyme

5. "Jack fell <u>from a higher to a lower place</u> and broke his crown." _____ — Nursery Rhyme

6. "The <u>bird with large staring eyes</u> and the Pussy-Cat went to sea." _____ — Edward Lear

Spelling Compound Words

Eyes and Ears

Word List

maybe

bedroom

lunchroom

into

something

nobody

doghouse

myself

inside

notebook

Word + Word = Compound Word

dog + house = doghouse

Say each word. Listen for the two words you hear in each word.

Study the spelling. Look for familiar words in each word. How many words do you see in each word?

Write the words.

1-10. Write the ten words. Circle each of the words that you find in the compound words.

1. may be
2. _____
3. _____
4. _____
5. _____
6. _____
7. _____
8. _____
9. _____
10. _____

Spelling Tip
Compound words are formed by joining two other words.

Words You Know

Complete the story with the correct words from the word list.

School Days

On school days I get up very early. There is _____ else up at this hour. I stay in my _____ and read for a while. Then I get dressed all by _____.

Before I leave, I always have _____ to eat. Sometimes I have toast, or _____ some cereal. While I eat, I hear scratching on the door. It is my dog, Blue. He sleeps in a _____ in our yard at night. I open the door and let him _____.

When it is time to leave, I get my things together. I check to make sure I have my pencil and _____. Most days I put my lunch _____ my backpack. Sometimes I like to buy lunch at school. Everyone in my class eats in the _____. At the door, I pat Blue and off I go!

Word Fun: Words That Tell Where

Inside tells where something happened. Circle the word in each pair that tells where.

1. out, every
2. with, below
3. full, down

4. upstairs, something
5. smart, around
6. across, first

Spelling Compound Words   109

Words You Know

Put the Pieces Together: Write the words from the word list that are spelled by fitting the pieces of the puzzles together. Only use each piece once.

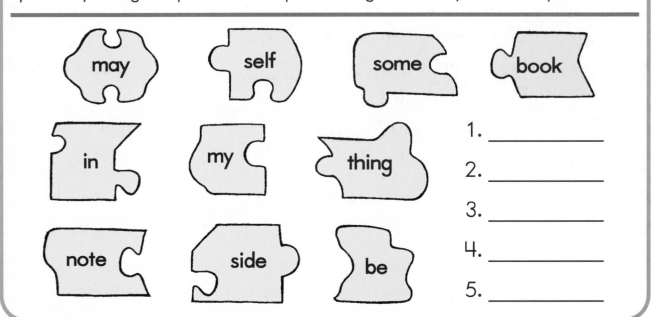

may   self   some   book

in   my   thing

note   side   be

1. _____
2. _____
3. _____
4. _____
5. _____

Join the Words: Write the words that are made by joining two words in each sentence into a compound word. Use the word list to help you.

6. I will eat my lunch in my room today.   _____

7. Did you find a note in your spelling book?   _____

8. You may fall on the steps, so please be careful.   _____

9. My dog likes to stay in the house at night.   _____

10 Make the bed in your room before you leave.   _____

11. There are no bones in the body of a worm.   _____

12. Take the box in the kitchen to the shed.   _____

Word List

maybe   bedroom   myself   notebook
nobody   dog-   into   inside
   lunchroom   something

Proofreading Practice

Here is Gator's description. Circle the three words that are spelled wrong. Write each word correctly in the spaces below.

I walked to school by miself. It rained all day so
we stayed inside for recess We ate in the new
lunchrum Our teacher gave us a spelling notbook.
I made a new friend. I was busy so the day passed
by very quickly.

1. _____   2. _____   3. _____

4-5. Two periods were not put at the ends of sentences.
Correct the mistakes.

Review

Write a word from the word list for each clue below.

6. It is where you eat at school.   _____

7. You write things in it.   _____

6. You say this instead of **yes** or **no**.   _____

Spelling Number Words

Eyes and Ears

Word List

one

two

three

four

five

six

seven

eight

nine

ten

Say each word. Listen for familiar vowel and consonant sounds.

Study the spelling. Do you see some short and long vowel spellings you have studied? Do you see any unusual spellings?

Write the words.
1-10. Write the ten words. Circle the short and long vowel spellings you see.

1. ___One___   6. _____

2. _____   7. _____

3. _____   8. _____

4. _____   9. _____

5. _____   10. _____

Spelling Tip
Some number words have common spellings. Others must be remembered.

Words You Know

Complete the story with the correct words from the word list.

Just the Numbers, Please

Ten students in Miss Kitty's class were divided into two teams. Five children were on each team.

Here are the ten math problems they had to solve:

Two plus five is   _____.

Three plus five is   _____.

Six minus four is   _____.

Seven minus six is   _____.

Four plus six is   _____.

Nine minus four is   _____.

Three plus one is   _____.

Eight minus five is   _____.

Two plus four is   _____.

Six plus three is   _____.

Each student had to give the answer to one problem. How many would you have gotten right? Would you have helped your team to win?

Word Fun: Homophones

Some number words are **homophones**. Homophones are words that sound alike but are spelled differently. Write the word with the correct spelling and meaning to complete each sentence.

1. I go _____ school. (to, two)   3. We _____ lunch. (eight, ate)

2. Here is _____ hat. (one, won)   4. Pass _____ cups. (for, four)

Words You Know

Look and Count: Write the word from the word list that tells how many of each thing listed below you find in the picture.

1. _____ balls   3. _____ pictures   5. _____ fish

2. _____ clocks   4. _____ books

Tell How Many: Write the words from the word list that answer the questions.

6. How many fingers are on one hand? _____

7. How many toes are on both feet? _____

8. How many ears does a dog have? _____

9. How many sides are in a △? _____

10. How many noses are on one face? _____

11. How many people are in two pairs of twins? _____

12. How many days are in one week? _____

13. How many letters are in the word **classroom**? _____

14. What is six plus two? _____

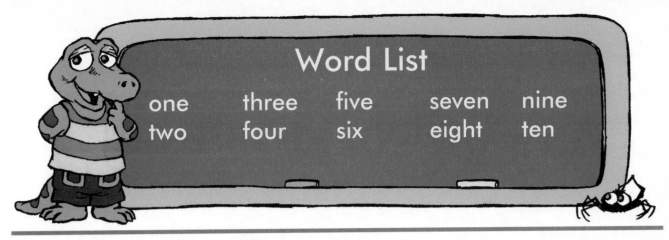

Word List

one	three	five	seven	nine
two	four	six	eight	ten

Proofreading Practice

Here is Little Critter's story. Circle the three words that are spelled wrong. Write each word correctly in the spaces below.

My name is Little Critter. I am sevin years old. I am in the second grade. I love animals. I have for pets. I have won dog. I have a cat and a frog. I also have a goldfish. When I am eight years old, I will get a new pet. I hope it is a horse!

1. _____   2. _____   3. _____

Review

Write a word from the word list to anwer each question using the pictures.

4. How many teeth?

_____

6. How many sides?

5. How many legs?

_____

_____

Speller Dictionary

A

and Mom and Dad like to sing.

any 1. Sit in any chair.
2. Do you feel any better?
3. Any of these books will help.

art Painting, sculpture, composing, and writing are forms of art.

ask Little Critter will ask Mom.

aunt My aunt is married to my uncle.

B

baby 1. The baby is learning how to walk.
2. She is the baby of the family.

bad 1. I watched a bad television show.
2. Tiger felt bad when his team lost the game.

bait Grandpa uses worms for bait.

band The band played at the Critterville parade.

barn The cows stay in the barn when it is cold.

bath 1. Blue needs a bath.
2. The bath was too hot.

bedroom I keep my toys and books in my bedroom.

bend We will bend the wire to make a shape.

bird All birds have feathers, and most birds can fly.

blast We saw the spacecraft blast off.

blend This drink is a blend of fruit juices.

blink Dad blinked when the light flashed.

block The house was built of blocks of stone.

blow 1. A heavy blow with a

hammer drove the nail into the board.
2. The wind blows the leaves all around. 3. Blow out the candles!

boat Grandpa paddled the boat across the lake.

book Gabby loves to read books.

boot Boots are usually made of leather or rubber.

brag Don't brag about how smart you are.

brick Bricks are used in building.

bright 1. The bright light hurt Grandma's eyes.
2. Let's paint the chair a bright color.

broom We used the broom to sweep up the dirt.

brother Molly has a twin brother.

C

came Mrs. Critter came to Little Critter's game.

camp The camp is near a river.

cane He needs a cane to walk.

cart Carts are usually pulled by horses, mules, or oxen.

choke That tight collar could choke the dog.

clash The Critterville band ended the parade music with a clash of cymbals.

clown The clown had a funny red nose.

coat 1. I have a new coat.
2. We will coat the house with paint.

come Does your dog come to you when you call it?

cry The loud noise made the baby cry.

D

dark At midnight, it is dark outside.

dear 1. You are a dear friend.
2. You are a dear to come over and help.

deep 1. I don't swim in the deep end of the pool.
2. The princess fell into a deep sleep.

deer A male deer has antlers.

desk My desk at school is next to Tiger's.

die Flowers die when it gets cold outside.

dirt Malcolm washed the dirt off his hands before dinner.

dock Grandpa pulled the boat to the dock.

does Little Critter does all his homework.

dog Dogs are related to coyotes, wolves, and foxes.

doghouse Blue sleeps in his doghouse.

down 1. Kitty climbed down from the tree.
2. Baby birds' feathers are called down.

dream Little Critter had a dream that he was flying.

drip Be careful not to drip paint on the rug.

drive Mom will drive us to the pet store.

drove Dad drove us to Grandpa's house.

drum Her brother plays the drum in the Critterville School band.

dry 1. Dad put on some dry clothes after the rain storm.
2. I will dry the dishes.

dump I dumped my books on the table.

dye Mom wants to dye the blue curtains red.

E

each Each player gets a turn.

egg The chick hatched from its egg.

eight Four plus four is eight.

every Every student in Miss Kitty's class is here today.

F

family Little Critter has a nice family.

farm Grandpa grows corn and beans on his farm.

fast Tiger can run very fast.

fat 1. That hippo is fat!
2. All that money makes your wallet fat.

father Mr. Critter is Little Critter's father.

fed I fed the animals in the morning.

fight 1. Two dogs had a fight over the bone.
2. I will fight this cold.

first 1. George Washington was the first president.
2. She was first in her class.

five Bun Bun's little sister can count to five.

fix Mom can fix the broken chair.

flash A flash of lightning lit the sky for an instant.

flop Little Critter couldn't wait to flop into bed.

fly 1. A fly can be bothersome.
2. Some birds fly south.
3. The pilot will fly the plane.

fog The thick fog made driving dangerous.

food People need food to live.

foot 1. Little Critter's foot hurt after the game.
2. I am one foot taller than my brother.

for 1. We worked for two hours.
2. This box is for my race cars.

four Dogs and cats have four legs.

free We set the bird free.

frisky Blue is a frisky dog.

frog Frogs are closely related to toads.

full 1. The box is full.
2. We had a house full of guests for the party.

G

gas (gasoline) We filled the car's tank with gas.

get I hope to get a scooter for my birthday.

girl There are ten girls in my class.

give I give my sister my old toys.

glad Mom was glad we helped out.

glass 1. May I please have a glass of orange juice?
2. Windows are made of glass.

go I like to go to the Critterville Zoo.

goat Goats have short horns and a tuft of hair under their chins that looks like a beard.

gone The oranges are all gone.

good 1. The food at this restaurant is good.
2. We had a good time.
3. Blue was a good dog at the vet.
4. I have a good excuse for being late.

got I got a present for my mom.

grade Next year I will be in third grade.

grand The king and queen live in a grand palace.

grandfather My grandfather loves to go fishing.

grandmother My grandmother makes the best pies.

grape We like to eat grapes for a snack.

grin Gator had a grin on his face when he won the game.

H

hand My hand hurt after playing catch.

hard 1.They work hard on the farm.
2. It rained so hard yesterday that the roads flooded.

has My friend has a new bicycle.

hat On cold days Molly wears her wool hat.

hay Grandma feeds hay to the cows.

hid I hid the surprise outside.

hide Kitty always hides when it thunders.

his Maurice is proud of his sister.

hook 1. Little Sister put her sweater on the hook.
2. I hooked Blue's leash to his collar.

horn 1. Deer and sheep have horns.
2. Dad honks the car horn when he gets home.

horse Horses are graceful animals.

house Gabby's family asked us to come to their house for dinner.

I

if 1. If you are hungry, have a snack.
2. I can go if I finish my homework first.

inside The inside of the house was dark.

into 1. We walked into the house.
2. Little Sister bumped into the door.

J

job 1. Mr. Stork's job is to run the toy store.
2. It's my job to feed and walk my dog.
jog Mom and Dad jog in the park for exercise.
jump Gator had to jump to catch the baketball.
just You just missed the plane!

K

kick 1. I can kick the ball far.
2. Tiger gave the soccer ball a hard kick.
kiss 1. I kiss Grandma and Grandpa good-bye.
2. Little Sister gave Mom a kiss.

L

lap Molly sat on her grandmother's lap.
last Little Critter was last in line.

light 1. The empty box was light.
2. A light rain fell.
3. The sun gives off light.
list The spelling words are in a list.
live They live in our neighborhood.
lock The front door has a lock.
log The pioneer family used logs to build their cabin.
long It's a long way from our school to the zoo.
look 1. Take a look at my new bicycle!
2. Miss Kitty has a cheerful look.
3. I looked at Maurice's stamp collection.
4. Look at the camera and smile!
lose 1. I hate when I lose my pencil.
2. The team won't lose the game.
lost I lost my jacket on the playground.
lot 1. There are a lot of cars on this road.
2. We play baseball in an empty lot.
loud 1. The jet engine

made a loud noise.
2. Dad's green and purple tie is very loud.

luck   Wish me luck!

lunchroom   I eat in the lunchroom every day at school.

M

mad   I was mad when I missed the Super Critter Show.

man.   The boy grew up to be a strong man.

map   He studied the map before his trip.

mask   I wore a mask in the school play.

maybe   I don't agree with you, but maybe you are right.

meal   Breakfast is my favorite meal.

meat   Mom cooks meat for dinner sometimes.

meet   1. We won first place in the swim meet.
2. We will meet them at the train station.

met   I met my new teacher.

milk   I always have milk with my dinner.

mix   1. We mix flour and sugar when we bake.
2. Oil and water don't mix.

moon   The moon seems to shine because it reflects light from the sun.

more   1. A gallon is more than a quart.
2. Blue always wants more to eat.

mother   My mother is a doctor.

much   There isn't much lemonade left.

mud   Blue had mud on his paws.

must   1. I must return this book.
2. People must eat to live.
3. They must have forgotten.

myself   1. I am proud of myself.
2. I haven't been myself since I broke my arm.

N

night   The baby slept seven nights without crying.

nine   There are nine

players on Tiger's baseball team.

nobody I rang the doorbell, but nobody answered.

nose I breathe through My nose.

notebook We brought our notebooks to school.

now 1. Now, I have to walk home.
2. Eat your food now.

O

off 1. A button fell off my jacket.
2. I broke off a piece.

one There is only one cookie left.

our Our house is on Critter Lane.

out I turned on the faucet, and water gushed out.

owl Owls eat mice, frogs, snakes, and insects.

P

pack 1. Go pack your suitcase.
2. I see a large pack of wolves in the field.

pail I brought my pail and shovel to the beach.

park We play ball in the park near our home.

pat I pat my dog when he obeys.

pin 1. I wore my heart pin on my collar.
2. I will pin my ribbon to my shirt.

pine We have three pine trees in our yard.

plan Our plan for Saturday is to go to the beach.

plate I put plates on the table for Mom.

plot 1. The pirates made a plot to steal the gold.
2. That movie has an exciting plot.

plum The tree has red plums.

plus Two plus two is four.

pond There are fish in the pond.

pool Gabby's cousins have a pool.

pull I pull my wagon down the street.

push 1. I pushed the cart through the market.
2. We had to push

through the crowd.

put   Put the box on the table.

R

raise   1. I raised the flag.
2. Don't raise a commotion.
3. The worker got a raise in pay.

rake   Use the rake on the cut grass.

read   I learned to read when I was in first grade.

rest   1. She took a rest after working.
2. I rest when I feel sick.

ride   1. We took a ride.
2. We tried all the rides at the fair.
3. He rides his bicycle.

right   1. The student gave the right answer.
2. Telling the truth was the right thing to do.

rip   1. I ripped my pants on the fence.
2. You have a rip in your shirt.

road   The workers paved the road.

rock   Molly has a rock collection.

rode   I rode the bus to school yesterday.

room   1. There was no room to park the car.
2. Our house has seven rooms.

row   1. Grandpa will row the boat.
2. A row of trees was planted in front of the house.

rub   Rub some lotion on your hands.

rude   I don't want to be rude to anyone.

rug   There is a rug in front of the fireplace.

rust   There is rust on the old gate.

S

sack   Place the sack of potatoes on the floor.

sand   I like to dig in the sand.

say   What did you say?

sea   The crew struggled to keep the ship afloat in the rough sea.

see   1. I see better with

glasses.

2. I see what you mean.

seen Those old shoes have seen much wear.

send Send the card to Mr. Molini.

seven There are seven puppies.

shame 1. He felt shame for not telling the truth.

2. It was a shame that we lost.

sharp That knife has a sharp blade.

sheep They made the sheep's wool into yarn.

shine The stars shine at night.

shirt My favorite shirt has red buttons.

shock The parents never got over the shock of the storm.

shore 1. We walked along the shore.

2. The sailors were glad to be back on shore.

short 1. The grass is short.

2. The car stopped short.

shut 1. We shut the window. 2. The door shut behind me.

sick Little Sister is sick with the flu.

sight 1. The group caught sight of the cabin.

2. My glasses helped my sight.

sister Maurice has a sister named Molly.

six We know six games.

slam 1. The door closed with a slam.

2. Please don't slam the door.

sled Gator's sled flew over the snow.

slick 1. The horse had a slick coat.

2. The boat left a slick of oil on the water.

slide 1. Let's slide down the hill in our sleds.

2. I like to go down the slide.

slip 1. I wrote my friend's telephone number on a slip of paper.

2. Don't slip on the ice!

snack I had a snack after school.

snow Maurice and Molly like to watch the snow fall.

soap Use soap when you give Blue a bath.

something 1. Your house looks something like ours.

2. Something is wrong

with our car.

song   The words of the song are pretty.

soon   1. Come to visit us again soon.
2. Our guests arrived too soon.

sound   1.The owl made a strange sound.
2. The bell sounded at nine o'clock.

space   The planet Earth orbits in space.

speech   1. Animals do not have the power of speech.
2. I heard the president's speech.

speed   1. She ran with great speed.
2. We speed down the hill on our sleds.

spin   1. The top spins fast.
2. Spiders spin webs.

spot   1. That park is a nice spot for a picnic.
2. There is a spot of ketchup on your shirt.

spy   1. He is a spy for the government.
2. I spy on Little Sister.

stack   I ate a big stack of pancakes.

start   What time does the game start?

stick   1. Put a stick of wood on the fire.
2. Stick the stamp on the letter.

sting   1. A bee sting hurts.
2. I don't want that bee to sting me!

stuck   Little Critter stuck a letter in the mailbox.

such   I have never seen such weather.

T

take   1. Gator can take the book.
2. The nurse takes my temperature.

teach   My neighbor teaches swimming lessons.

team   Tiger's soccer team practices every day.

ten   Ten pennies equals one dime.

test   Miss Kitty gave us a spelling test on Friday.

thank   1. I thanked Molly for helping me. 2. I have you to thank for a wonderful day.

them   I ran to my grandparents and hugged them.

thin I could see through the thin wrapping paper.

thing 1. That was a kind thing to say.
2. What is that thing on Blue's nose?

those I like those kind of apples.

three The three of us will play the game.

tip The tips of the fingers are very sensitive.

toad A toad has rough, dry skin and spends most of its time on land rather than water.

took Mom took me to the dentist.

tooth The dentist said my teeth were nice and white.

town Critterville is a friendly town.

trade I will trade my new marble for your baseball.

train 1. Some trains carry passengers.
2. I will train my dog to do tricks.

tree A tree has branches and leaves.

trick 1.The magician did many tricks.
2. We tried to trick Malcolm.

trip 1. Don't trip on the rug!
2. Mom and Dad are taking a trip.

truck There are boxes in the truck.

tube A garden hose is a long tube.

tug 1. Blue tugs on his leash.
2. Suddenly I felt a tug on the fishing line.

tune 1. We hummed the tune.
2. The band played a few popular tunes.

two There were two birds on the wire.

U

uncle My uncle will go with me.

us The neighbors invited us to dinner.

V

very I am very sorry that

you are not feeling well.

W

were   We were at home all day.

what 1. What is today's date? 2. They knew what I was thinking.

wheel   The car has four wheels.

where   Where did they go?

while 1. Did anyone call while I was away?
2. We stopped and rested for a while.

whisker   Cats and dogs have whiskers.

who 1. Who gave you that pen?
2. The student who wrote that story is a good writer.

why   Why are you laughing?

wide 1. The house has a wide porch.
2. The room is ten feet wide.

wing   The bird has a broken wing.

with 1. I went with my friends.

2. We need someone with good skills for the job.

Y

yard   We have a vegetable garden in our yard.

yet   I have never yet been late.

your   Let's meet tomorrow at your house.

Z

zoo   Malcolm went to the zoo to learn about animals.

Spelling the Short a Sound

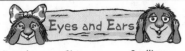
Eyes and Ears

Sound	Sign	Spelling
short a	/a/	map hat

Word List

lap
nap
hat
map
has
pat
mad
gas
fat
bad

Say each word. Listen for the short a sound in **map** and **hat**.

Study the spelling. How is the short a vowel spelled?

Write the words.
1-10. Write the ten words. Circle the letter that spells the short vowel sound.

1. l@p   6. p@t
2. n@p   7. m@d
3. h@t   8. g@s
4. m@p   9. f@t
5. h@s   10. b@d

Spelling Tip
The short a sound is often spelled a.

Words You Know

Complete the story with the correct words from the word list.

A Day with Grandpa

Grandpa __has__ a small farm. I like to sit on his __lap__ and hear stories.

One day, Grandpa took me for a ride. First, we put __gas__ in the car. Then, Grandpa read the __map__. Grandpa forgot his __hat__. He wasn't __mad__. He gave me a __pat__ on the back. I ran to get Grandpa's hat. I almost tripped over Grandpa's __fat__ cat! The cat was taking a __nap__ on the floor.

It's too __bad__ we were running late. We only went for a short ride.

Word Fun: Word Families

Change the first letter in each word to spell a word from the word list. Write the words.

1. bat   __hat, pat, or fat__   3. cat   __hat, pat, or fat__
2. cap   __lap nap, or map__   4. lad   __mad or bad__

Words You Know

Fill in the Letters: Write the two words from the word list that fit each puzzle.

1-2.

	m	
	a	
b	a	d

5-6.

	g	
	a	
h	a	s

3-4.

m	a	p
	a	
	t	

7-8.

	f	
n	a	p
	t	

Unscramble and Spell: Write a word from the word list by changing the order of the following letters.

9. ash   __has__   11. tap   __pat__
10. pal __lap__   12. pan   __nap__

Pair Up the Words: Write the missing word that goes with each word.

13. good and __bad__   14. coat and __hat__

15. oil and __gas__

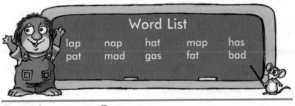

Word List

| lap | nap | hat | map | has |
| pat | mad | gas | fat | bad |

Proofreading Practice

Here is Little Critter's story about a bad day. Circle the three words that are spelled wrong. Write each word correctly in the spaces below.

Monday was a (bed) day. I spilled milk on my (lup.) After that I sat on my new hat. Then I could not find the state I live in on the (mep). I was sad that day.

1. __bad__   2. __lap__   3. __map__

✏ Review

Write a word from the word list for each clue below.

4. It makes a car run.   __gas__
5. You wear this on your head.   __hat__
6. You can find your town on this. __map__

Spelling the Short i Sound

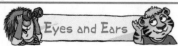

Word List

if
fix
pin
his
mix
rip
kiss
hid
tip
milk

Sound	Sign	Spelling
short i	/i/	pin fix

Say each word. Listen for the short i sound in **pin** and **fix**.

Study the spelling. How is the short vowel spelled?

Write the words.
1-10. Write the ten words. Circle the letter that spells the short vowel sound.

1. (i)f
2. f(i)x
3. p(i)n
4. h(i)s
5. m(i)x

6. r(i)p
7. k(i)ss
8. h(i)d
9. t(i)p
10. m(i)lk

Spelling Tip
The short i sound is often spelled **i**.

8   Spelling the Short i Sound

Complete the story with the correct words from the word list.

A Real Treat

Gator loves ___his___ mom. He wanted to do something that would make her happy. So he went into the kitchen to ___fix___ her lunch.

Gator had to do many things to get ready. He had to ___rip___ off the leaves from a head of lettuce. Next, he cut off the ___tip___ of a carrot. Then he had to ___mix___ the cooked vegetables. Finally, he poured her a glass of ___milk___ .

When Gator was finished, he tried to ___pin___ a flower on his mom's napkin. Then he ___hid___ a note under her dish. His mom gave him a big ___kiss___ .

Could you make lunch ___if___ you tried?

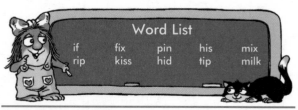

Word Fun: Opposites

Write the opposite of each word. Each answer will have a short i sound.

1. her ___his___   3. break ___fix___   5. out ___in___
2. small ___big___   4. stand ___sit___

Spelling the Short i Sound   9

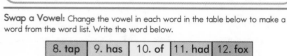

Look and Write: Write the words from the word list that fit each clue.

Two words that end with the letter **x**.

1. ___fix___   2. ___mix___

Two words that end with two consonants.

3. ___kiss___   4. ___milk___

The word that has the word **in** in it.

5. ___pin___

Two words that rhyme with **lip**.

6. ___rip___   7. ___tip___

Swap a Vowel: Change the vowel in each word in the table below to make a word from the word list. Write the word below.

8. tap	9. has	10. of	11. had	12. fox
tip	his	if	hid	fix

Use the Dictionary: Words in a dictionary are arranged in ABC order. Look at the first letter in each word below. Write the word in each group that would come first in ABC order.

13. rip   pin   mix ___mix___   15. rip   milk   kiss ___kiss___
14. hid   tip   if ___hid___   16. milk   if   pin ___if___

10   Spelling the Short i Sound

Word List

if	fix	pin	his	mix
rip	kiss	hid	tip	milk

Proofreading Practice

Here is Gator's list. Circle the words that are spelled wrong. Write each word correctly in the spaces below.

1. (Fex) a broken toy (ef) I can.
2. Play a game.
3. Give Mom a hug and a (kis.)

1. ___fix___   2. ___if___   3. ___kiss___

Review

Write a word from the word list that fits each group of words.

4. hug, wave, hello, good-bye, ___kiss___

5. juice, water, tea, ___milk___

6. hers, yours, mine, theirs, ___his___

Spelling the Short i Sound   11

Spelling the /o/ and /ô/ Sounds

Eyes and Ears

Word List
log
got
dog
job
lot
fog
flop
spot
jog
off

Sound	Sign	Spelling
short o	/o/	job
	/ô/	log

Say each word. Listen for the vowel sounds in job and log. Note the sign for each sound.

Study the spelling. How are these sounds spelled?

Write the words.
1-10. Write the ten words. Circle the letter that spells the vowel sound.

1. l(o)g
2. g(o)t
3. d(o)g
4. j(o)b
5. l(o)t
6. f(o)g
7. fl(o)p
8. sp(o)t
9. j(o)g
10. (o)ff

Spelling Tip
The short o and /ô/ sounds are often spelled o.

12   Spelling the /o/ and /ô/ Sounds

Words You Know

Complete the story with the correct words from the word list.

Gabby's Job
Gabby has a new ___job___ after school. She ___got___ the job last week. Gabby is happy because she will now be able to save some money. She wants to buy some new pet fish.

Gabby's job is a ___lot___ of fun. She takes a big black and white ___dog___ for walks. She has to take the dog out every day in sun, rain, or ___fog___.

Sometimes Gabby takes the dog to a safe ___spot___ and runs around with it. Other times she sits by herself on a ___log___ while the dog runs ___off___ by itself. Maybe one day she will ___jog___ with the dog. Then they both will ___flop___ down under a tree to rest.

Word Fun: More Than One
Add -s to each word to show more than one.
1. one log, two ___logs___
2. one spot, two ___spots___
3. one pot, two ___pots___
4. one hog, two ___hogs___
5. one frog, two ___frogs___
6. one tot, two ___tots___

Spelling the /o/ and /ô/ Sounds   13

Words You Know

Listen and Write: Write the word from the word list that has the same ending sound as the picture words. Circle the word that ends with two consonants.

cup   web   leaf
1. flop   2. job   3. (off)

Rhyme and Answer: Write the missing word. It will rhyme with the underlined word.

4. A place for a bed is a <u>cot</u> ___spot___ .
5. A wooden toy for a pet is a <u>dog</u> ___log___ .
6. A yard for children is a <u>tot</u> ___lot___ .

Add Another Word: Think how the words in each group are alike. Write the word from the word list that belongs in each group.

7. snow, sleet, rain, ___fog___
8. fish, cat, bird, ___dog___
9. walk, skip, run, ___jog___
10. hot, spot, lot, ___got___

14   Spelling the /o/ and /ô/ Sounds

Word List
log	got	dog	job	lot
fog	flop	spot	jog	off

Proofreading Practice
Here is Little Critter's letter. Circle the three words that are spelled wrong. Write each word correctly in the spaces below.

Dear Grandma and Grandpa,
    I got a (jeb). It is a (lat) of work. I wash our dog. I get off every (spat) of dirt. My family likes my work. So does my dog.
                                Love,
                                Little Critter

1. ___job___   2. ___lot___   3. ___spot___

4 - 5. Two periods are missing. Correct the mistakes.

Review
Write a word from the word list to complete each sentence. The missing word will rhyme with the underlined word.

6. An oven or fire is a <u>hot</u> ___spot___ .
7. A pig who "barks" is a <u>hog</u> ___dog___ .
8. When you have a little, you do <u>not</u> have a ___lot___ .

Spelling the /o/ and /ô/ Sounds   15

131

Spelling the Final /k/ Sound

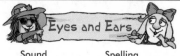
Eyes and Ears

Word List
rock
kick
sack
dock
pack
sick
stack
lock
stick
snack

Sound	Spelling
/k/	lock

Say each word. Listen for the last sound you hear in **lock**.

Study the spelling. How is this sound spelled?

Write the words.
1-10. Write the ten words. Circle the letters that spell the last sound.

1. r o (ck)
2. k i (ck)
3. s a (ck)
4. d o (ck)
5. p a (ck)

6. s i (ck)
7. st a (ck)
8. l o (ck)
9. st i (ck)
10. sn a (ck)

Spelling Tip
A final /k/ sound is spelled **ck**.

Words You Know

Complete the story with the correct words from the word list.

A Busy Afternoon
Today I will go down to the boat __dock__ with my friend, Tiger. There is a lot of trash on the dock. People should put their trash in the garbage. All the cans left around make me __sick__! We will __stack__ them in a pile and take them to the dump.

Later we can __kick__ a ball around the yard. Then we can climb to the top of the big __rock__. We will __snack__ on apples and nuts. Tiger and I will __pack__ the food in a bag. I will carry the paper __sack__ in my backpack. I will bring a long __stick__ to help me walk. I hope I will not forget to __lock__ my house door before I go.

Word Fun: Word Meaning
Write the word from the word list that means the same or almost the same as each word.

1. pole ___stick___
2. bag ___sack___
3. stone ___rock___

4. pile ___stack___
5. ill ___sick___
6. treat ___snack___

Words You Know

Change Numbers to Letters: Use the code below to help you write six words from the word list.

Number	1	2	3	4	5	6	7	8	9	10
Code	a	c	d	i	k	l	o	p	s	t

1. 6-7-2-5 ___lock___
2. 9-4-2-5 ___sick___
3. 9-10-4-2-5 ___stick___
4. 5-4-2-5 ___kick___
5. 9-10-1-2-5 ___stack___
6. 8-1-2-5 ___pack___

Read and Write: Write the words from the word list that fit each clue.

Three words that begin with two consonants.

7. ___stack___   8. ___stick___   9. ___snack___

Four words that have a short **a** sound.

10. ___sack___ 11. ___pack___ 12. ___stack___ 13. ___snack___

Three words that have a short **o** sound.

14. ___rock___   15. ___dock___   16. ___lock___

Two words that begin like **stop**.

17. ___stack___   18. ___stick___

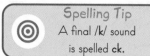

Word List
rock   kick   sack   dock   pack
sick   stack   lock   stick   snack

Proofreading Practice

Here is Tiger's list. Circle the three words that are spelled wrong. Write each word correctly in the spaces below.

Things I Like to Do
1. (Kik) a football.
2. Hit a ball with a (stik).
3. Fish off the (dok).
4. Climb a rock.

1. ___kick___   2. ___stick___   3. ___dock___

Review
Write a word from the word list to complete each sentence.

4. Grandma doesn't feel well. She feels ___sick___.

5. The best after school ___snack___ is an apple.

6. Maurice put one block on top of the other.

   He made a ___stack___.

Spelling the /nd/ and /st/ Sounds

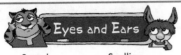
Eyes and Ears

Sound	Spelling
/nd/	ha**nd**
/st/	lo**st**

Word List

sand
pond
lost
just
and
last
list
band
fast
hand

Say each word. Listen for the last sound your hear in **hand** and **lost**.

Study the spelling. How are these sounds spelled?

Write the words.
1-10. Write the ten words. Circle the letters that spell the last sound.

1. sa(nd)
2. po(nd)
3. lo(st)
4. ju(st)
5. a(nd)

6. la(st)
7. li(st)
8. ba(nd)
9. fa(st)
10. ha(nd)

Spelling Tip
The /nd/ and /st/ sounds are spelled **nd** and **st**.

Words You Know

Complete the story with the correct words from the word list.

My Lost Cat

Fluffy is my pet cat. I cannot find her anywhere. She is ___lost___. I saw her ___just___ this morning after breakfast. Fluffy and I were near the frog ___pond___ in my backyard. I was digging in the ___sand___. She was sitting next to me looking around.

I held out my ___hand___. "Here, Fluffy!" I called. But she ran away as ___fast___ as she could. Maybe she saw another cat or a dog or a mouse! That was the ___last___ time I saw her.

She has a white ___band___ around her neck. She has white paws ___and___ a white tail. I made a ___list___ of places to look for her. I hope that I will find her soon. I miss my pet!

Word Fun: Words That Describe

Write the words from the word list that the describing words tell something about.

1. big, loud   ___band___
2. hot, white   ___sand___

3. left, right   ___hand___
4. deep, small   ___pond___

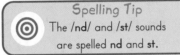
Words You Know

Make New Words: Take the first two letters and the last two letters of each word to make a word from the word list. For example: sa̲lt + wi̲nd = sand

1. pool + land   ___pond___
2. life + mist   ___list___
3. love + fist   ___lost___

4. hall + kind   ___hand___
5. fair + rust   ___fast___

Listen to the Sounds: Write the word from the word list that begins with the same sound as each picture.

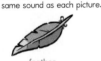
feather
6. ___fast___

heart
8. ___hand___

sandwich
10. ___sand___

jam
7. ___just___

book
9. ___band___

Keep Looking: Write the word from the word list that you find in each of these words.

11. unjust   ___just___
12. breakfast   ___fast___
13. grand   ___and___

14. listless   ___list___
15. everlasting   ___last___

Word List

sand	lost	and	list	fast
pond	just	last	band	hand

Proofreading Practice

Here is Gabby's poster. Circle the three words that are spelled wrong. Write each word correctly in the spaces below.

PLEASE HELP!
Have you seen Toby? He is (lawst.) He is a brown and white horse. He has a white (bandd) down his back. Toby was last seen near the (pend.)

1. ___lost___   2. ___band___   3. ___pond___

4. One question mark is missing at the end of a question. Correct the mistake.

Review

Write a word from the word list that is the opposite of each word below.

5. found   ___lost___
6. first   ___last___
7. slow   ___fast___

Spelling the Short e Sound

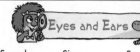
Eyes and Ears

Word List
egg
fed
met
them
rest
bend
yet
test
went
send

Sound	Sign	Spelling
short e	/e/	fed

Say each word. Listen for the short e sound in **fed**.

Study the spelling. How is the vowel sound spelled?

Write the words.
1-10. Write the ten words. Circle the letter that spells the short e sound.

1. ⓔgg   6. bⓔnd
2. fⓔd   7. yⓔt
3. mⓔt   8. tⓔst
4. thⓔm   9. wⓔnt
5. rⓔst   10. sⓔnd

Spelling Tip
The short e sound is often spelled e.

Words You Know

Complete Little Critter's letter with the correct words from the word list.

Dear Grandma and Grandpa

Dear Grandma and Grandpa,

The other day I watched a robin build a nest. After the mother bird sat on it awhile, a tiny ___egg___ hatched. The baby robin poked its head out and ___met___ its mother.

The mother robin did not sit and ___rest___. She ___went___ away to find food. Then she came back and ___fed___ the baby a worm. She had to ___bend___ way down to feed it.

Of course, the baby robin cannot leave the nest ___yet___. Some day it will ___test___ its wings and try to fly.

I drew a picture of ___them___. I will ___send___ it to you. Will you come here soon to see the robins and their nest?

Love,
Little Critter

Word Fun: Past Tense

Add **-ed** to each word to show the past.
Now I **pick**. A day ago I **picked**.

1. rest   ___rested___   4. rent   ___rented___
2. test   ___tested___   5. peck   ___pecked___
3. spell   ___spelled___

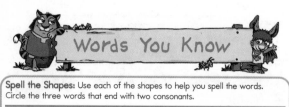
Words You Know

Spell the Shapes: Use each of the shapes to help you spell the words. Circle the three words that end with two consonants.

● = r   ▲ = m   ■ = h   ⌴ = s
▬ = t   ↑ = n   ◆ = d   ↓ = e

1. ▲↓▬   ___met___   4. ■■↓▲   ___them___
2. ▬↓⌴▬   (___test___)   5. ●↓⌴▬   (___rest___)
3. ⌴↓↑◆   (___send___)

Use the Dictionary: Where would you look to find these six words in the dictionary? Use the chart below to help you.

went   met   egg   fed   yet   bend

abcdefghi	jklmnopq	rstuvwxyz
look in the beginning of the dictionary	look in the middle of the dictionary	look at the end of the dictionary

6. Which three words are found at the beginning of the dictionary?

___egg___   ___fed___   ___bend___

7. Which word is found in the middle?

___met___

8. Which two words are found at the end of the dictionary?

___went___   ___yet___

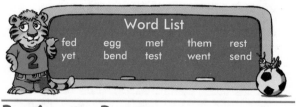
Word List

fed	egg	met	them	rest
yet	bend	test	went	send

Proofreading Practice

Here is Molly's poem. Circle the three words that are spelled wrong. Write each word correctly in the spaces below.

I (mat) some little blue jays,
So I gave (tham) all some hay.
They built a small and cozy nest.
They worked hard and did not (rist!)

1. ___met___   2. ___them___   3. ___rest___

✏ Review

Write a word from the word list to complete each sentence.

4. Tiger is still not here. He hasn't come ___yet___.

5. Each chicken has an ___egg___ in its nest.

6. Little Sister got a good grade on the spelling ___test___.

Spelling the Short u Sound

Eyes and Ears

Sound	Sign	Spelling
short u	/u/	m**u**d

Word List

us
mud
rub
tug
luck
must
rug
shut
rust
stuck

Say each word. Listen for the short u sound in **mud**.

Study the spelling. How is the vowel sound spelled?

Write the words.
1-10. Write the ten words. Circle the letter that spells the short u sound.

1. ⓤs
2. mⓤd
3. rⓤb
4. tⓤg
5. lⓤck

6. mⓤst
7. rⓤg
8. shⓤt
9. rⓤst
10. stⓤck

Spelling Tip
◎ The short u sound is often spelled **u**.

Words You Know

Complete the story with the correct words from the word list.

Car Wash

Every Saturday I ___must___ wash our family car. My little sister helps me. We wash off the dirt and ___mud___. We try not to get the inside of the car wet. We always make sure to ___shut___ the windows before we wash it. Sometimes we find some ___rust___ on the hood. But we cannot ___rub___ it off with a rag.

After we wash the car, we shake the sand from the ___rug___ on the floor. Sometimes the seat gets ___stuck___. One good ___tug___ is all it takes to move it.

With ___luck___ we can finish the job in an hour. It makes ___us___ feel good when the job is done. The car looks good, too!

Word Fun ➤ Word Meaning

Write the words from the word list that mean the same or almost the same as each word below.

1. dirt ___mud___
2. pull ___tug___
3. close ___shut___

4. we ___us___
5. carpet ___rug___
6. scrub ___rub___

Words You Know

Circle the Words: Write the word in each sentence that has a word from the word list hidden in it. Then circle the word.

1. You can see a tugboat in the harbor. ___tug___
2. There are many rubber boots in the store. ___rub___
3. I will go on the bus with Bun Bun. ___us___
4. They are shutting the windows. ___shut___
5. We are lucky to be such good friends. ___luck___

Break the Code: Use ABC order to fill in the missing letter in each group. Then write the word that is spelled with the underlined letters.

s_t_u t_u_v f_g_h = tug

6. r_s_t s_t_u t_u_v b_c_d j_k_l   ___stuck___
7. q_r_s t_u_v r_s_t s_t_u   ___rust___
8. l_m_n t_u_v c_d_e   ___mud___
9. q_r_s t_u_v f_g_h   ___rug___
10. l_m_n t_u_v r_s_t s_t_u   ___must___

Rhyme and Spell: Write two words from the word list that rhyme with each word below.

duck
11. ___luck___
12. ___stuck___

bug
13. ___tug___
14. ___rug___

dust
15. ___must___
16. ___rust___

Word List

| mud | us | rub | rug | luck |
| rug | must | shut | rust | stuck |

Proofreading Practice

Here are Malcolm's directions. Circle the three words that are spelled wrong. Write each word correctly in the spaces below.

1. Shet the doors and close the windows.
2. Wash the car and rob with a rag.
3. Shake the dirt from the rog.

1. ___shut___   2. ___rub___   3. ___rug___

Review

Write a word from the word list for each meaning below.

4. wet dirt ___mud___
5. a cover for the floor ___rug___
6. cannot move ___stuck___

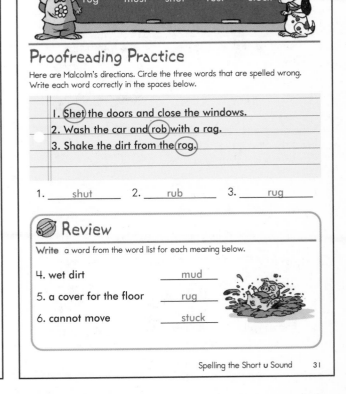

Spelling Words with dr, tr, and gr

Eyes and Ears

Word List
drip
grin
tree
drum
grade
trip
drive
grand
truck
drove

Sound	Spelling
/dr/	drive
/tr/	truck
/gr/	grade

Say each word. Listen for the first two sounds in **drive**, **truck**, and **grade**.

Study the spelling. How are the first two sounds spelled?

Write the words. The blends, **dr**, **tr** and **gr** are listed below. Write the words that belong under each consonant blend.

dr	tr	gr
drip	tree	grin
drum	trip	grade
drive	truck	grand
drove		

Spelling Tip
The /dr/, /tr/, and /gr/ sounds are spelled dr, tr, and gr.

Words You Know

Complete the story with the correct words from the word list.

The Family Truck

Malcolm is in the second ___grade___. His family owns a gray pickup ___truck___. They park it in the driveway under a shady ___tree___.

One day oil began to ___drip___ from it. So the truck had to be taken to be fixed. It is still a ___grand___ truck. Malcolm likes to ride in it. One day when he is older, Malcolm wants to ___drive___ a truck just like it.

Last summer Malcolm went with his family on a ___trip___. They ___drove___ a long way to see some friends. Their friends gave Malcolm a present when he got there. They knew that Malcolm likes music so they gave him a big ___drum___. Malcolm gave them a big ___grin___ in return. He was so happy with his surprise.

Word Fun: Word Endings

Each word below has an ending. Write the word from the word list you find in each word.

1. dripped	drip	4. trucker	truck
2. trees	tree	5. drummers	drum
3. grinning	grin	6. grades	grade

Words You Know

Figure It Out: Write the word that is spelled after you add and subtract letters.

1. grove - gr + dr = ___drove___
2. land - l + gr = ___grand___
3. sip - s + tr = ___trip___
4. win - w + gr = ___grin___
5. ship - sh + dr = ___drip___

grove - gr + dr = ?

Think and Write: Write a word from the word list for each clue below.

6. Someone might tell you to beat it. ___drum___
7. It could go from ear to ear. ___grin___
8. You cannot hear its bark, but you can see it. ___tree___
9. You need a car before you can do this. ___drive___
10. An "A" is a good one. ___grade___

Be an Author: Write the missing word in each book title. Use the word list to help you. Be sure to start with a capital letter.

Learn How to ___ a Car

Maps for ___ Drivers

How to Have a ___ Time

11. ___Drive___   12. ___Truck___   13. ___Grand___

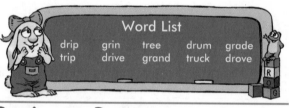

Word List

drip	grin	tree	drum	grade
trip	drive	grand	truck	drove

Proofreading Practice

Here is Little Critter's story. Circle the three words that are spelled wrong. Write each word correctly in the spaces below.

Last summer my family took a (trap) We had a (grond) time. We (drov) to the lake. it was a long drive, but we had lots of fun.

1. ___trip___   2. ___grand___   3. ___drove___

4 - 5. Two capital letters were not used at the beginning of sentences. Correct the mistakes.

Review

Write a word from the word list that fits each group of words below.

6. bark, leaf, trunk, ___tree___
7. car, van, bus, ___truck___
8. horn, piano, guitar, ___drum___

Spelling Words with gl, bl, and pl

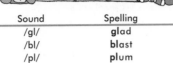

Eyes and Ears

Sound	Spelling
/gl/	**gl**ad
/bl/	**bl**ast
/pl/	**pl**um

Word List
blast
glad
plan
blend
plus
glass
plum
blink
plot
block

Say each word. Listen for the first two sounds in **glad**, **blast**, and **plum**.

Study the spelling. How are the first two sounds spelled?

Write the words. The blends **gl**, **bl**, and **pl** are listed below. Write the words that belong under each consonant blend.

gl	bl	pl
glad	blast	plan
glass	blend	plus
	blink	plum
	block	plot

Spelling Tip
The /gl/, /bl/, and /pl/ sounds are spelled gl, bl, and pl.

Words You Know

Complete Little Sister's letter with the correct words from the word list.

Dear Grandma and Grandpa

Dear Grandma and Grandpa,

We __plan__ to have a picnic on the Fourth of July. I am very __glad__. Everyone on our __block__ will come. Mom is going to make __plum__ pudding. We will also bring a __glass__ of lemonade for everyone. We will __blend__ fresh lemons, water, and sugar to make it.

Our town will have fireworks that night. The show will be held on a big __plot__ of land. We will watch the fireworks __blast__ off. Don't __blink__ or you'll miss them!

Fireworks __plus__ a picnic will add up to a good time for everyone. I hope you can come to our picnic.

Love,
Little Sister

Word Fun: More Than One

Add -**es** to words ending with -**s** to show more than one.
one **glass**, two **glasses**

1. one dress, two __dresses__   3. one plus, four __pluses__

2. one boss, three __bosses__   4. one class, six __classes__

Words You Know

Look and Write: Write the words from the word list which have the same beginning sound as each picture.

1. __plant__   5. __blast__   9. __glad__
2. __plus__   6. __blend__   10. __globe__
3. __plum__   7. __blink__
4. __plot__   8. __block__

Use the Dictionary: An entry word is the word you look up in a dictionary. A definition tells you what the word means. Many entry words have more than one meaning.
Look up the word **plot** in your Speller Dictionary to answer the questions.

11. What is the entry word? __plot__

12. What is the sentence given for the first meaning? __The__ __pirates made a plot to steal the gold.__

13. What is the sentence given for the second meaning? __That__ __movie has an exciting plot.__

14. Which meaning is the **main idea of a book?** __second meaning__

15. Which two words come after **plot**? __plum__   __plus__

Word List
| blast | glad | plan | blend | plus |
| glass | plum | blink | plot | block |

Proofreading Practice

Here is Little Sister's invitation. Circle the three words that are spelled wrong. Write each word correctly in the spaces below.

Please (plain) to come to our picnic on the Fourth of July. I will be so (glod). We will have food (plas) games.

1. __plan__   2. __glad__   3. __plus__

4 - 5. Two periods were not put in at the end of sentences. Correct the mistakes.

Review

Write the sentences below. Replace the underlined word with a word from the word list.

6. Molly was <u>happy</u> that Gabby could come to the party.
   __Molly was glad that Gabby could come to the party.__

7. First put in the milk, then <u>mix</u> in the eggs.
   __First put in the milk, then blend in the eggs.__

8. Three <u>and</u> three equals six.
   __Three plus three equals six.__

Spelling Words that End with **sk**, **mp**, and **ng**

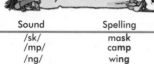
Eyes and Ears

Word List

mask	
camp	
long	
ask	
sting	
dump	
wing	
desk	
song	
jump	

Sound	Spelling
/sk/	mask
/mp/	camp
/ng/	wing

Say each word. Listen for the ending sounds in **mask**, **camp**, and **wing**.

Study the spelling. How are the ending sounds spelled?

Write the words. The blends **sk**, **mp**, and **ng** are listed below. Write the words that belong under each consonant blend.

sk	mp	ng
mask	camp	long
ask	dump	sting
desk	jump	wing
		song

Spelling Tip
The /sk/, /mp/, and /ng/ sounds are spelled **sk**, **mp**, and **ng**.

40   Spelling Words that End with **sk**, **mp**, and **ng**

Words You Know

Complete Little Critter's list with the correct words from the word list.

Things to Do

When you __camp__ in the woods, there are some things you must remember to do. Here is a list Little Critter wrote at his __desk__.

1. Be sure to __ask__ someone where you can put your tent.
2. Bugs may __sting__, so bring a spray.
3. Take a __long__ walk every day.
4. Look for a blackbird with red feathers on its __wing__.
5. When you spot a raccoon, look for the __mask__ that seems to be on its face.
6. Watch a frog __jump__ over a log.
7. Sing a happy camp __song__ every night.
8. Remember to __dump__ your trash in a can before you leave.

Word Fun: Adding -ing

Add **-ing** to the end of each word below. Write the new word.

9. camp + ing = __camping__   12. jump + ing = __jumping__
10. dump + ing = __dumping__   13. ask + ing = __asking__
11. sting + ing = __stinging__

Spelling Words that End with **sk**, **mp**, and **ng**   41

Words You Know

Finish the Rhyme: Write the word from the word list that rhymes with each underlined word.

1. Put a <u>stamp</u> on the letter to __camp__.
2. Why did you toss the <u>pump</u> in the __dump__?
3. We sang a <u>song</u> that was too __long__.
4. Please <u>ask</u> them if they have a __mask__.
5. When the car went over the <u>bump</u> it made me __jump__.

Compare and Write: Write the missing word that finishes the sentence.

6. A fish has a fin. A bird has a __wing__.
7. A rabbit can hop. A frog can __jump__.
8. An artist paints a picture. A singer sings a __song__.
9. A snake can bite. A bee can __sting__.
10. A teacher can write on a chalkboard.
    A student can write at a __desk__.

Ask and Tell: Read each pair of sentences. Write the word **ask** if the sentence is a question. Write the word **tell** if the sentence gives an answer.

11. What is wrong with that bird?   __ask__
12. I think it has a broken wing.   __tell__
13. My desk is near the window.   __tell__
14. Where is your desk in the classroom?   __ask__

42   Spelling Words that End with **sk**, **mp**, and **ng**

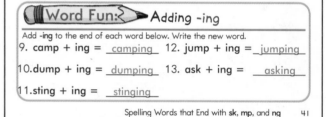

Word List

mask	camp	long	ask	sting
dump	wing	desk	song	jump

Proofreading Practice

Here are Gabby's rules. Circle the four words that are spelled wrong. Write each word correctly in the spaces below.

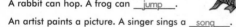

1. Do not (junp) on the bed.
2. Take your trash to the (domp).
3. Write a (log) letter home every week.
4. Get help for a bee (steng).

1. __jump__   2. __dump__   3. __long__   4. __sting__

Review

Write a word from the word list to finish each sentence. The missing word will rhyme with the underlined word.

5. It rained on our tents.
   Now we have a <u>damp</u> __camp__.
6. Don't play that music.
   That is the <u>wrong</u> __song__.
7. The bird had a <u>string</u> caught on its __wing__.

Spelling Words that End with **sk**, **mp**, and **ng**   43

138

Spelling the Long **a** Sound

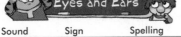
Eyes and Ears

Sound	Sign	Spelling
long a	/ā/	rake bait hay

Word List
- rake
- bait
- say
- cane
- pail
- hay
- plate
- raise
- came
- grape

Say each word. Listen for the long **a** sound in **rake**, **bait**, and **hay**.

Study the spelling. How is the long **a** vowel spelled in each word?

Write the words.
1-10. Write the ten words. Circle the letters that spell the long **a** sound.

1. r(a)k(e)
2. b(ai)t
3. s(ay)
4. c(a)n(e)
5. p(ai)l
6. h(ay)
7. pl(a)t(e)
8. r(ai)se
9. c(a)m(e)
10. gr(a)p(e)

Spelling Tip
The long **a** sound can be spelled a_e, ai, and ay.

44   Spelling the Long a Sound

Words You Know

Complete the story with the correct words from the word list.

Gone Fishing

Maurice and I like to fish. We made our own fishing rods. We used an old walking ___cane___ for one fishing rod. For the other rod, we used the handle of an old garden ___rake___. It had been used to gather grass and ___hay___. We used worms for ___bait___.

Some days we have no fish to carry home in our ___pail___. But I would ___say___ that we are lucky most of the time. When we ___raise___ the fishing line out of the water, a fish is usually on the hook.

One day we ___came___ home with ten fish. At supper, two fresh fish were on each ___plate___. They tasted great with some ___grape___ juice.

Word Fun: Same Sound, Different Meaning

Circle the two words in each group with the same sound but different spellings and meanings.

1. (pail), (pale), peal
2. tall, (tail), (tale)
3. (hey), hi, (hay)
4. (hole), hold, (whole)
5. (plain), plan, (plane)

Spelling the Long a Sound   45

Words You Know

Picture This Scene: Write the six words from the word list you can find in the picture.

1. rake
2. bait
3. pail
4. hay
5. plate
6. grape

Write the Rhyme: Write the words from the word list that rhyme with each word.

7. drape   grape
8. bake   rake
9. wait   bait   plate
10. pay   say   hay
11. game   came
12. gate   plate   bait
13. mail   pail
14. lane   cane

Dictionary Skills: Entry words in the dictionary are in ABC order. When entry words begin with the same letter, you must look at the second letter. Write the words in each group in ABC order.

15. plate pole pail   pail   plate   pole
16. came crane clay   came   clay   crane
17. rust raise reel   raise   reel   rust
18. coat cane crab   cane   coat   crab

46   Spelling the Long a Sound

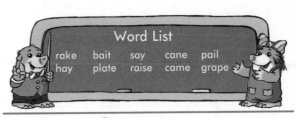
Word List

rake	bait	say	cane	pail
hay	plate	raise	came	grape

Proofreading Practice

Here is Maurice's newspaper story. Circle the four words that are spelled wrong. Write each word correctly in the spaces below.

> Yesterday two big fish were caught off the town dock. Worms were used for (bate). The fish were so big they could not fit on a dinner (plat). Everyone (kame) to see them. Some (sey) they were the biggest fish they have ever seen!

1. bait   2. plate   3. came   4. say

5 - 6. Two periods are missing at the ends of sentences. Correct the mistakes.

Review

Write a word from the word list to complete each sentence.

7. Gator used worms for ___bait___ and caught six fish.

8. Grandma is here. Please ___say___ hello.

9. Little Sister piled the food on her ___plate___.

Spelling the Long a Sound   47

Spelling the Long e Sound

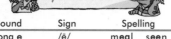

Eyes and Ears

Sound	Sign	Spelling
long e	/ē/	meal seen

Word List

read
each
seen
wheel
team
deep
meal
treat
dream
sheep

Say each word. Listen for the long **e** sound in **meal** and **seen**.

Study the spelling. How is the long **e** sound spelled in each word?

Write the words.
1-10. Write the ten words. Circle the two letters that spell the long **e** sound.

1. r (ea) d
2. (ea) ch
3. s (ee) n
4. wh (ee) l
5. t (ea) m
6. d (ee) p
7. m (ea) l
8. tr (ea) t
9. dr (ea) m
10. sh (ee) p

Spelling Tip
The long **e** sound is spelled **ea** and **ee**.

Words You Know

Complete the story with the correct words from the word list.

Dreamland

Little Critter likes to __read__ books. He likes make-believe stories the best. One night he fell into a __deep__ sleep. He had a strange __dream__. He dreamed about a girl and boy in one of the books.

The girl and boy had to watch over a herd of __sheep__ all the time. They found a surprise late one day when they were about to eat their evening __meal__. The surprise was a real __treat__.

They found out that __each__ bean on their dinner plates was magic! Every bean became a __wheel__ that went around and around! On top of the wheels was a beautiful coach. It was pulled by a __team__ of white horses.

The girl and boy laughed, climbed into the coach, and rode into the sky. They were never __seen__ again.

What a dream!

Word Fun: Same Spelling, Different Meaning

Write the word from the box that fits the two meanings below.

beat	seal	deep	meal

1. breakfast/ground corn   __meal__
2. animal/close an envelope   __seal__
3. hit again/mix together   __beat__
4. far down/rich in color   __deep__

Words You Know

Unscramble the Words: Circle the three scrambled words in the poem. Write the words correctly in the spaces below.

Try to (reda) a book (chae) and every day,
A few pages at a time will get you on your way.
Many new friends you will surely meet,
It will be a lot of fun and a real (eattr!)

1. __read__   2. __each__   3. __treat__

Write the Rhyme: Write the word from the word list that answers the question and rhymes with the underlined word.

4. What is a round hub? a <u>steel</u> __wheel__
5. What is a very long nap? a __deep__ <u>sleep</u>
6. What is lunch for a sea animal? a <u>seal</u> __meal__
7. What is a winning sports group? a __dream__ <u>team</u>

Look in All Directions: Circle the six words from the word list you find hidden in the letter square.

s	v	w	x	a	d
e	t	e	a	m	e
e	e	a	c	h	e
n	s	h	e	e	p
d	r	e	a	m	w

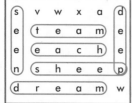

Word List

read	each	seen	wheel	team
deep	meal	treat	dream	sheep

Proofreading Practice

Here is Little Sister's book report. Circle the three words that are spelled wrong. Write each word correctly in the spaces below.

My favorite book is about shep. They live on a big farm. I red some pages ech day. It helps me learn about animals and how to treat them.

1. __sheep__   2. __read__   3. __each__

Review

Write a word to complete each sentence. The missing word will rhyme with the underlined word.

4. A great rest is a __deep__ <u>sleep</u>.
5. A ten-cent lunch is a <u>deal</u> on a __meal__.
6. Cold lemonade on a hot day is a __treat__ in the <u>heat</u>.

Spelling the Long i Sound

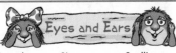
Eyes and Ears

Sound	Sign	Spelling
long i	/ī/	wide dry night

Word List

- pine
- night
- cry
- fight
- wide
- fly
- light
- sight
- dry
- right

Say each word. Listen for the long **i** sound in **wide**, **dry**, and **night**.

Study the spelling. How is the long **i** sound spelled in each word?

Write the words.
1-10. Write the ten words. Circle the letters that spell the long **i** sound.

1. p i n e
2. n igh t
3. cr y
4. f igh t
5. w i d e
6. fl y
7. l igh t
8. s igh t
9. dr y
10. r igh t

Spelling Tip
The long **i** sound can be spelled i_e, y, and igh.

Words You Know

Complete the story with the correct words from the word list.

Dear Tiger

Dear Tiger,

Do you want to go for a plane ride with me? In the daytime, we will see many things because it is __light__. We can __fly__ over houses and trees. We will soar over the long, __wide__ river below us. We will swoop low over a __pine__ forest. At __night__, we will see the moon and the stars and the Critterville city lights.

We will take turns sitting near the window. That way we will not __fight__ over the seat. Do not get scared and __cry__ if the ride gets bumpy. Just __dry__ your eyes. Look to both the left and __right__. I know you will enjoy each wonderful __sight__!

Your pal,
Little Critter

Word Fun: Opposites

Write the word that means the opposite of each word below.

1. day ___night___
2. left ___right___
3. wet ___dry___
4. narrow ___wide___
5. laugh ___cry___
6. heavy ___light___

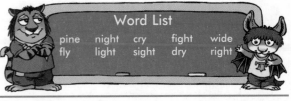
Words You Know

Look and Write: Write the words from the word list that fit each clue.

1-2. Do not ___fly___ your kite at ___night___.

5-6. Turn on the ___light___ to help your ___sight___.

9. Children should share their toys rather than ___fight___.

3-4. All ___wide___ trucks keep to the ___right___.

7-8. Don't ___cry___! ___Dry___ your eyes.

Write the Words: Write the words from the word list that fit the descriptions.
Which three words end with long **i** spelled **y**?

10. ___cry___   11. ___dry___   12. ___fly___

Which two words end with vowel-consonant-vowel?

13. ___pine___   14. ___wide___

Dictionary Skills: Many words have more than one meaning. A dictionary lists all the meanings for a word. Read the pairs of meanings. Write the word that fits both meanings.

15. an insect with two wings/move through the air ___fly___

16. a lamp/not dark ___light___

17. good or correct/opposite of left ___right___

18. kind of tree/wish or long for something ___pine___

Word List

pine	night	cry	fight	wide
fly	light	sight	dry	right

Proofreading Practice

Here is Little Critter's weather report. Circle the four words that are spelled wrong. Write each word correctly in the spaces below.

Today will be fair and (dri) Clouds will move in at (nit). It will rain (rite) after midnight. Pilots should not (flie) their planes. Stay at home until the sky clears!

1. ___dry___   2. ___night___   3. ___right___   4. ___fly___

5 - 7. Three sentences do not begin with capital letters. Correct the mistakes.

Review

Write a word from the word list that means the opposite of each word below.

8. wet ___dry___

9. wrong ___right___

10. day ___night___

Spelling the Long o Sound

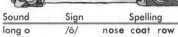
Eyes and Ears

Sound	Sign	Spelling
long o	/ō/	nose coat row

Say each word. Listen for the long o sound in **nose**, **coat**, and **row**.

Study the spelling. How is the long o sound spelled in each word?

Write the words.
1-10. Write the ten words. Circle the letter that spells the long o sound.

Word List

coat
blow
nose
boat
row
those
goat
soap
snow
toad

1. c (oa) t
2. bl (ow)
3. n (o) s (e)
4. b (oa) t
5. r (ow)

6. th (o) s (e)
7. g (oa) t
8. s (oa) p
9. sn (ow)
10. t (oa) d

Spelling Tip
◎ The long o sound can be spelled o_e, oa, and ow.

Words You Know

Complete the story with the correct words from the word list.

Gabby's Report

My report is about an animal called the mountain __goat__. It leaps from rock to rock like a __toad__ jumping frome log to log. It races over the hills like a __boat__ gliding over water. It can even cling to the side of a cliff with __those__ strong hooves. It would be as hard to catch as a wet bar of __soap__.

Ice and __snow__ often cover the rocks of its home. Sometimes a cold wind will __blow__. The goat has a thick __coat__ of fur to keep it warm.

The mountain goat has to poke its __nose__ around to find plants to eat. If it is lucky, it will find a __row__ of moss on the hillside.

Word Fun: Compound Words

Add each word to a word from the word list to make a compound word.

soap + suds = __soapsuds__   3. rain + coat = __raincoat__

1. sail + boat = __sailboat__   4. snow + ball = __snowball__

2. nose + dive = __nosedive__   5. toad + stool = __toadstool__

Words You Know

Pair Them Up: Write the two missing words in each sentence. Use the picture clues to help you.

1-2. **Here is a** __toad__
on a bar of __soap__.

5-6. **There is a** __goat__
in the __snow__.

3-4. **This is a** __boat__
you can __row__.

Think and Write: Write words from the word list that match each clue.
Write three words that end with a long o sound.

7. __blow__   8. __row__   9. __snow__

Write two words that end with the first sound you hear in **zebra**.

10. __nose__   11. __those__

Write the shortest word from the list.

12. __row__

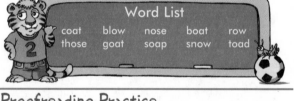
Word List

coat	blow	nose	boat	row
those	goat	soap	snow	toad

Proofreading Practice

Here is Gator's ad for a trip to the mountains. Circle the four words that are spelled wrong. Write each word correctly in the spaces below.

In summer, (roe) a boat or go hiking. Perhaps you will see a mountain (gote) or a toad. In winter, play in the (snoe). Then sit by the fire when the night winds (bloo).

1. __row__   2. __goat__   3. __snow__   4. __blow__

Review

Write a word from the word list for each clue below.

5. This is used in the shower.   __soap__

6. This is what the wind does.   __blow__

7. This is part of the face.   __nose__

142

Spelling the /ü/ Sound

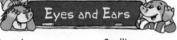
Eyes and Ears

Sound	Spelling
/ü/	tune moon

Word List

tube
zoo
boot
food
tune
pool
soon
rude
moon
room

Say each word. Listen for the /ü/ sound in **tune** and **moon**.

Study the spelling. How is the /ü/ sound spelled in each word?

Write the words.
1-10. Write the ten words. Circle the two letters that spell the vowel sound.

1. t(u)b(e)   6. p(oo)l
2. z(oo)   7. s(oo)n
3. b(oo)t   8. r(u)d(e)
4. f(oo)d   9. m(oo)n
5. t(u)n(e)   10. r(oo)m

Spelling Tip
The /ü/ sound can be spelled u_e and oo.

Words You Know

Complete the story with the correct words from the word list.

Visit the Critterville Zoo

Have you ever gone to the Critterville _Zoo_ to see the animals there? You can watch the seals swim in a _pool_. They have a lot of _room_ to swim and dive. They like to play with a ball and an old tire _tube_. Sometimes they will clap their flippers if someone plays them a _tune_.

Every day at noon, Ms. Dingo, the zoo keeper, gives them _food_. Sometimes a big seal will take fish from a little seal. Do you think that is _rude_?

If you stay until night, you will see the _moon_. But you must go home _soon_. If not, Ms. Dingo might _boot_ you out!

Word Fun: Place Words

Town and **room** are words that name places. Circle the place word in each group.
1. (pool), boot, soon
2. tune, (zoo), paper
3. food, (room), clock
4. (house), glove, table
5. stool, (park), rude
6. June, (lake), tube

Words You Know

Think and Write: Write the word from the word list that is missing from each sentence.

1. **Person** is to **neighborhood** as **animal** is to ___zoo___.
2. **Head** is to **hat** as **foot** is to ___boot___.
3. **Day** is to **sun** as **night** is to ___moon___.
4. **Skate** is to **rink** as **swim** is to ___pool___.
5. **Book** is to **words** as **song** is to ___tune___.
6. **Drink** is to **water** as **eat** is to ___food___.

Be a News Reporter: Write the missing word that finishes each newspaper headline. Be sure to begin each word with a capital letter.

7.	8.	9.	10.
Town To Get A New Swimming _Pool_	Spaceship Lands on the _Moon_	Hungry People Get _Food_	Panda Bear Given to the _Zoo_

Use the Dictionary: Write each set of entry words in the order you find them in the dictionary.

11.	rude	room	rail	_rail_	_room_	_rude_
12.	stem	soon	sun	_soon_	_stem_	_sun_
13.	moon	mule	mean	_mean_	_moon_	_mule_
14.	tube	trip	take	_take_	_trip_	_tube_
15.	zoo	zebra	zero	_zebra_	_zero_	_zoo_

Word List

tube	zoo	boot	food	tune
pool	soon	rude	moon	room

Proofreading Practice

Here are Little Sister's questions. Circle the three words that are spelled wrong. Write each word correctly in the spaces below.

1. Do you like working at the (zu)?
2. What (fod) do you feed the lions?
3. How often do you clean the seal (poole)?

1. ___zoo___   2. ___food___   3. ___pool___

4 - 5. Two question marks were not put at the ends of questions. Correct the mistakes.

Review

Write a word from the word list that fits each group of words below.

6. sun, stars, ___moon___
7. shoe, slipper, ___boot___
8. music, song, ___tune___

Spelling Words with **wh** and **sh**

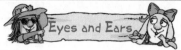

Word List
what
clash
shame
why
shine
flash
shock
where
shore
while

Eyes and Ears

Sound	Spelling
/hw/ or /w/	what
/sh/	shine flash

Say each word. Listen for the first sound you hear in **what**. Listen for the first sound you hear in **shine** and the last sound you hear in **flash**. Note the signs for these sounds.

Study the spelling. How are these sounds spelled in the words?

Write the words.
1-4. Write the four words with the beginning /hw/ or /w/ sound spelled **wh**.
5-10. Write the six words with the beginning and ending /sh/ sound spelled **sh**.

1. what
2. where
3. while
4. why

5. clash
6. shame
7. shine
8. flash
9. shock
10. shore

Spelling Tip
The /hw/ or /w/ sound is often spelled **wh**.
The /sh/ sound is often spelled **sh**.

Words You Know

Complete the story with the correct words from the word list.

The Critterville School Band

Can you guess the reason _why_ Little Critter plays in the Critterville School Band? He loves to hear the _clash_ of the cymbals.

The places _where_ the band plays are always different. Once, they played as they marched along the _shore_ of a lake. They had lots of fun.

At first, the day was nice. Little Critter hoped the sun would _shine_ all day. Suddenly, it started to grow darker and darker. Then the band members saw a _flash_ of light! Soon after, they heard claps of thunder.

The storm came as a _shock_ to everyone. The band members were all wet. "_What_ a _shame_!" said the band leader.

Word Fun: Compound Words

Add a word from the word list to each word below. Write the compound word.
mean + while = _meanwhile_   3. **sun** + _shine_ = _sunlight_
1. _flash_ + **light** = _flashlight_   4. _what_ + **ever** = _whatever_
2. **some** + _where_ = _somewhere_   5. _shore_ + **line** = _shoreline_

Words You Know

Find a Rhyme: Write the word from the word list that rhymes with the underlined word or part of a word in each sentence.

1. Can you <u>smile</u> for a little _while_?
2. I feel <u>fine</u> when the sun does _shine_.
3. Is there a book<u>store</u> near the sea _shore_?
4. When I fell off the <u>rock</u>, it was a big _shock_.

Look and Spell: Write the words from the word list that answer the questions.
Which four words have the same beginning sound as ?

5. _shame_   6. _shine_   7. _shock_   8. _shore_

Which two words have the same ending sound as ?

9. _clash_   10. _flash_

Which four words have the same beginning sound as ⊕ ?

11. _what_   12. _where_   13. _while_   14. _why_

Write the Questions: Write a question to go with each answer. Be sure to use **what**, **where**, or **why** in your question. Remember to end each question with a question mark. Circle each question word that you use.

15. Question: _Where are they?_
    Answer: They are at the shore.
16. Question: _What are you looking for?_
    Answer: We are looking for seashells.
17. Question: _Why do you need shells?_
    Answer: We need the shells for the science fair.

Word List
| what | clash | shame | why | shine |
| flash | shock | where | shore | while |

Proofreading Practice

Here are the words to a song that Molly wrote. Circle the three words that are spelled wrong. Write each word correctly in the spaces below.

Oh, (wy) did you move?
Oh, (wher) are you now?
It is such a (sham).
Nothing is the same without you.

1. _why_   2. _where_   3. _shame_

Review

Write a word from the word list for each clue below.

4. a question word that rhymes with <u>air</u>   _where_

5. a bright light that rhymes with <u>dash</u>   _flash_

6. land that is next to a lake or sea that rhymes with <u>more</u>

shore

144

Spelling Words with ch and th

Eyes and Ears

Word List

much
thing
such
choke
tooth
thank
bath
thin
teach
with

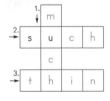

Sound	Spelling
/ch/	choke
/th/	thank with

Say each word. Listen for the first sound you hear in **choke** and **thank**. Listen for the last sound you hear in **with**. Note the signs for these sounds.

Study the spelling. How are the /ch/ and /th/ sounds spelled in the words?

Write the words.
1-4. Write the four words spelled with the beginning and ending /ch/ sound.
5-10. Write the six words spelled with the beginning and ending /th/ sound.

1. <u>much</u> 5. <u>thing</u>
2. <u>such</u> 6. <u>tooth</u>
3. <u>choke</u> 7. <u>thank</u>
4. <u>teach</u> 8. <u>bath</u>
  9. <u>thin</u>
  10. <u>with</u>

Spelling Tip
The /ch/ and /th/ sounds are spelled **ch** and **th**.

Words You Know

Complete the story with the correct words from the word list.

Growing Up

On Saturday I woke up <u>with</u> all my teeth in my mouth. But the <u>thing</u> that would change that was an apple.

I had so <u>much</u> to do that day. First, I wanted to <u>teach</u> my dog, Blue, a new trick. While we were playing, Blue ran into a big mud puddle. So I had to give him a <u>bath</u>. Blue did not <u>thank</u> me after I was done!

Then I stopped for lunch. After eating my sandwich, I ate an apple. I try to eat every meal so I will not be too <u>thin</u>!

All of a sudden, my <u>tooth</u> fell out when I bit into the apple. It was <u>such</u> a surprise! I was lucky that I did not swallow my tooth and <u>choke</u>. I hope my new tooth will grow in soon!

Word Fun: Word Endings

Add **-er** to the end of each word to show a **person who**.
buy + er = buyer

1. teach + er = <u>teacher</u> 4. catch + er = <u>catcher</u>

2. paint + er = <u>painter</u> 5. speak + er <u>speaker</u>

3. climb + er = <u>climber</u>

Words You Know

Finish the Puzzles: Fill in the words from the word list that fit each puzzle.

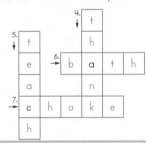

Hide and Seek: Write the words from the word list hidden in each ad.

8. <u>tooth</u> 9. <u>bath</u> 10. <u>with</u>

Buy two toothbrushes. Get one free.

THIS WEEK ONLY
All bathtubs on sale!

A treat without a fuss! Try new Snack Bars.

Use the Dictionary: A dictionary entry often gives a sample sentence to help explain a word's meaning. Look up the words below in the Speller Dictionary in the back of this book. Then write your own sentence for each of these words.

11. teach <u>Answers will vary.</u>
12. thank _____
13. bath _____
14. thing _____

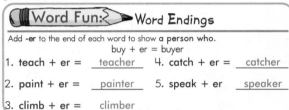
Word List

| much | thing | such | choke | tooth |
| thank | bath | thin | teach | with |

Proofreading Practice

Here is one of Malcolm's diary entries. Circle the four words that are spelled wrong. Write each word correctly in the spaces below.

Today I lost my front (tuth). I was taking a (bathe) and playing (whith) my toys. Suddenly it fell out. It was a strange (thig) to happen.

1. <u>tooth</u> 2. <u>bath</u> 3. <u>with</u> 4. <u>thing</u>

5 - 6. Two capital letters were not put at the beginning of sentences. Correct the mistakes.

Review

Write a word from the word list to fill in the blank in each pair of sentences. The missing word will rhyme with the underlined word.

7. Gator adds numbers when he is in the tub.
   Gator likes to do <u>math</u> in the <u>bath</u>.
8. A thick rug is a fat mat.
   A skinny needle is a <u>thin</u> pin.
9. Miss Kitty holds classes on the shore.
   She likes to <u>teach</u> at the <u>beach</u>.

Spelling the **Vowel + r** Sound

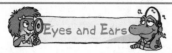
Eyes and Ears

Word List
farm
cart
dark
yard
art
barn
park
start
hard
sharp

Sound	Spelling
/är/	cart

Say each word. Listen for the **vowel + r** sound you hear in **cart**. Note the sign for this sound.

Study the spelling. How is the /är/ sound spelled in each word?

Write the words.
1-10. Write the ten words. Circle the letters that spell the /är/ sound.

1. f(ar)m
2. c(ar)t
3. d(ar)k
4. y(ar)d
5. (ar)t

6. b(ar)n
7. p(ar)k
8. st(ar)t
9. h(ar)d
10. sh(ar)p

Spelling Tip
◎ The /är/ sound may be spelled **ar**.

Words You Know

Complete the story with the correct words from the word list.

Down on the Farm
My Grandma and Grandpa live on a small __farm__. Like most farmers, they work very __hard__. They have to __start__ their chores early. Just after sunrise, they fill a __cart__ with feed for the pigs. Then they head for the __barn__ to milk the cows. Sometimes they work until it is __dark__.

On the weekends there are chores to do around the house. They have to cut the grass in the front __yard__. Of course, if the blades on the mower are __sharp__, the work goes faster.

Then they have time for some fun. Sometimes they like to go to the baseball __park__ to watch the home team play. Other times they take painting lessons at the __art__ school. They always like to keep busy.

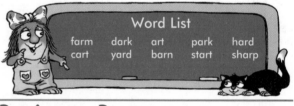
Word Fun: Comparing Things

The endings **-er** and **-est** are used to compare. **-Er** is used to compare two things. **-Est** is used to compare 3 or more things. Add **-er** and **-est** to each word.

hard   harder   hardest
1. sharp   sharper   sharpest
2. short   shorter   shortest
3. dark   darker   darkest
4. long   longer   longest
5. smart   smarter   smartest

Words You Know

Find and Change: Write the word from the word list that means the opposite of the underlined word.

1. It is <u>easy</u> to learn to roller skate.   hard
2. I painted the sky <u>light</u> blue in the picture.   dark
3. The blade on the knife is <u>dull</u>.   sharp
4. When will the bus <u>stop</u>?   start

Answer the Riddle: Write the words from the word list that answer the riddles.
5. I am a building. I am red. Horses and cows live in me.   barn
6. I am outside of a house or school.
   Sometimes children play on my grass.   yard
7. I have wheels. I carry things.   cart
8. I am land. People grow all kinds of crops on me.   farm
9. I am a big open space where people like to picnic.
   I have grass and trees. Sometimes I am in the city.   park

Finish the Book Cover: Write titles for the books using the following words: **art, farm, park.** Be sure to begin words in your book titles with capital letters.

10._____   11._____   12._____
                 Answers will vary   _____

Word List

| farm | dark | art | park | hard |
| cart | yard | barn | start | sharp |

Proofreading Practice

Here is Grandpa's list of chores. Circle the three words that are spelled wrong. Write each word correctly in the spaces below.

Farm Chores
1. Clean the (born)
2. Fill the (carte) with hay.
3. Rake the (yerd)
4. Feed the cows.

1. ___barn___   2. ___cart___   3. ___yard___

 Review

Write a word from the word list that fits each group of words.

4. night, black, shadow, ___dark___
5. pin, knife, ouch, ___sharp___
6. trees, swings, slides, ___park___

Spelling More Vowel + r Sounds

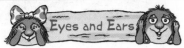
Eyes and Ears

Sound	Spelling
/ûr/	bird girl
/ôr/	horn for

Word List
girl
more
bird
horse
dirt
horn
short
first
for
shirt

Say each word. Listen for the **vowel + r** sound in **bird** and **girl**. Listen for the **vowel + r** sound in **horn** and **for**. Note the signs for these sounds.

Study the spelling. How are the /ûr/ and /ôr/ sounds spelled in each word?

Write the words.
1-5. Write the five words spelled with the /ûr/ sound.
6-10. Write the five words spelled with the /ôr/ sound.

1. girl
2. bird
3. dirt
4. first
5. shirt
6. more
7. horse
8. horn
9. short
10. for

Spelling Tip
The /ûr/ sound may be spelled **ir**.
The /ôr/ sound may be spelled **or**.

Words You Know

Complete the story with the correct words from the word list.

Early One Morning

Bun Bun woke up very early one morning when she heard a car __horn__. Nobody in the house was awake yet.

The young __girl__ got out of bed quickly. She put on a pair of pants and a __shirt__. She wanted to enjoy her __first__ day of summer vacation.

Bun Bun went outside after she fixed herself some breakfast. A small brown __bird__ greeted her with a song. She headed __for__ the barn. It was only a __short__ walk away.

Inside the barn, her __horse__ was waiting in a stall. He dug his hoof in the __dirt__ when he saw her. Bun Bun fed him some hay. She would give him some __more__ to eat later. Then she went riding.

Word Fun: Number Words

Number words tell **how many** and **which order**. Write the number word for each critter's place in line.   third   first   fifth   second   fourth

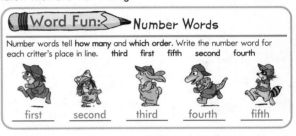

first   second   third   fourth   fifth

Words You Know

Be a Magician: Take away one word from the letters in each box. Write the word that is left.

1. Take away . Find a farm animal. | horhayse |
   horse

2. Take away ♪. Find something in a band. | honotern |
   horn

3. Take away . Find something to wear. | shiballrt |
   shirt

4. Take away . Find something to dig in. | dipailrt |
   dirt

5. Take away . Find a person. | gimaskrl |
   girl

Fill It In: Write the missing word. Be sure to begin each word with a capital letter.

6. For Sale
7. First Prize
8. Save More Here!
9. Tall Medium Short

Use the Dictionary: Many words have more than one meaning. Look up the word **horn** in the Speller Dictionary in the back of this book. Write two sentences using **horn**. Each sentence must use a different meaning for **horn**.

10. Answers will vary.

11. _____

Word List
girl   more   bird   horse   dirt
horn   short   first   for   shirt

Proofreading Practice

Here is Bat Child's plan. Circle the five words that are spelled wrong. Write each word correctly in the spaces below.

8:00-9:00	Make breakfast fer my family.
9:00-10:00	Buy a new red shert.
10:00-11:00	Go for a ride on my hors.
11:00-12:00	Repair the berd cage one mor time.

1. for
2. shirt
3. horse
4. bird
5. more

Review

Write a word from the word list that means the opposite of each word below.

6. boy   girl
7. last   first
8. tall   short

Easily Misspelled Words

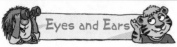
Eyes and Ears

Word List

does
gone
who
any
your
give
very
were
live
every

Say each word. Listen for the vowel and consonant sounds.

Study the spelling. Look for unusual or tricky spellings.

Write the words.
1-10. Write the ten words. Circle any spellings you find unusual. Try to remember them.

1. _does_
2. _gone_
3. _who_
4. _any_
5. _your_

6. _give_
7. _very_
8. _were_
9. _live_
10. _every_

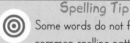

Spelling Tip
Some words do not follow common spelling patterns.

Words You Know

Complete the story with the correct words from the word list.

Road Race

Is there someone you know __who__ likes to run? Maybe it is a friend or someone in __your__ family. Maybe it is you! These days there are many people who are runners.

Running is a good way to keep fit. It __does__ not matter if you __live__ in the city or in the country. You can find a place to run __every__ day.

Some day you might like to enter a race. Are there __any__ races near where you live? Have you ever even __gone__ to a race? Some races are __very__ long. Each runner has to go over 26 miles to reach the finish line. The runners have to __give__ their best. How do you think you would feel if you __were__ in such a long race?

Word Fun: Same Spelling, Different Word

Write a word from the box that fits both blanks in each sentence.

live	does	close	wind

1. __Close__ a door _close_ to you.
2. I _live_ near a _live_ lion.
3. _Does_ the baby see the _does_?
4. _Wind_ a rope in the _wind_.

Words You Know

Add the Vowels: Fill in the missing vowels. Then write the words that are spelled. Be sure to remember that the letter y is sometimes used as a vowel. Use the word list to help you.

1. g o n e   gone
2. a n y   any
3. w e r e   were
4. g i v e   give
5. d o e s   does
6. e v e r y   every
7. l i v e   live
8. y o u r   your
9. wh o   who
10. v e r y   very

Answer and Write: Write the words from the word list that answer the questions.
11. Which word is a question word? __who__
12. Which word has the word **very** in it? __every__
13-15. Which three words end with a long **e** sound that is spelled **y**?
__any__   __every__   __very__

Find the Meaning: Write the words that can be used in place of the underlined words in each sentence.
16. Teachers <u>hand over</u> books to their students. __give__
17. I hope to read a book <u>each</u> week. __every__
18. The child is <u>so</u> happy with the bike. __very__
19. Would you like <u>some</u> grapes to eat? __any__
20. The painter has <u>moved</u> from the city. __gone__

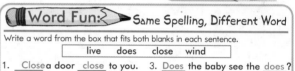
Word List

does	gone	who	any	your
give	very	were	live	every

Proofreading Practice

Here is Little Critter's postcard. Circle the four words that are spelled wrong. Write each word correctly in the spaces below.

Dear Tiger,
I am (vary) happy you won the race. Did they (giv) you a medal? Will you run in (eny) more races? (Wu) came in second?
Your pal,
Little Critter

1. __very__   2. __give__   3. __any__   4. __Who__

5 - 6. Two question marks were not put at the ends of questions. Correct the mistakes.

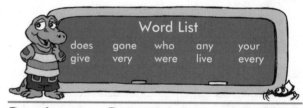
Review

Write a word from the word list to fill the blank in each pair of sentences.
7. Little Sister: Did you eat all the carrots?
   Bun Bun: Yes, I ate __every__ one of them.
8. Gator: Is this my jacket?
   Tiger: Yes, it is __your__ jacket.
9. Maurice: Did you like the popcorn?
   Molly: Yes, it was __very__ good!

Spelling Words with **br**, **fr**, and **tr**

Eyes and Ears

Sound	Spelling
/br/	brick
/fr/	frog
/tr/	trade

Word List

train

brag

free

trade

frog

brick

frisky

bright

trick

broom

Say each word. Listen for the first two sounds in **brick**, **frog**, and **trade**.

Study the spelling. How are the two beginning sounds spelled?

Write the words. The blends **br**, **fr** and **tr** are listed below. Write the words that belong under each consonant blend.

br	**fr**	**tr**
brag	free	train
brick	frog	trade
bright	frisky	trick
broom		

Spelling Tip
The /br/, /fr/, and /tr/ sounds are spelled **br**, **fr**, and **tr**.

Words You Know

Complete the story with the correct words from the word list.

My Pet Frog and I

I have a new pet ___frog___ . I found it in a pond. So I got it for ___free___ !

I try not to ___brag___ too much about my pet. It is a great frog. My frog is a ___bright___ green color. My frog is also very smart and very ___frisky___ . I plan to ___train___ my frog to do tricks. One ___trick___ it has already learned is to jump through a hoop that I am holding.

My friend, Little Critter, also has a pet frog. Sometimes we race our frogs on the red ___brick___ path in front of my house. We use the handle of a ___broom___ for the finish line.

Sometimes my frog wins. Sometimes Little Critter's frog comes in first. Either way, I would not ___trade___ my frog for anything. No, not ever!

Word Fun: Many Meanings

Some words have more than one meaning. Write the word from the word list that has both meanings.
1. railroad cars; to teach ___train___ 4. swap; job to make money ___trade___
2. shiny; smart ___bright___   5. fool or cheat; a clever act ___trick___
3. no cost; to set loose ___free___

Words You Know

Join the Pieces: Write the five words from the word list that are spelled by putting the bricks together. Be sure to use each brick part only one time.

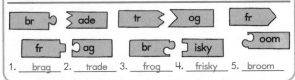

1. ___brag___ 2. ___trade___ 3. ___frog___ 4. ___frisky___ 5. ___broom___

Spell the Words: Write the words from the word list that fit the clues.

Two words that rhyme with **sick**.
6. ___brick___   7. ___trick___

Two words that have double vowels.
8. ___broom___   9. ___free___

The word that ends with long **e** spelled **y**.
10. ___frisky___

The word that rhymes with **fright**.
11. ___bright___

Put on Your Thinking Cap: Write the word that finishes each sentence.

12. You scrub with a mop. You sweep with a ___broom___ .
13. A bus travels on a road. A ___train___ travels on a track.
14. A fish can swim. A ___frog___ can hop.
15. Some houses are made of wood.
    Some houses are made of ___brick___ .

Word List

train	brag	free	trade	frog
brick	frisky	bright	trick	broom

Proofreading Practice

Here is Tiger's story. Circle the three words that are spelled wrong. Write each word correctly in the spaces below.

I have a new pet frog. It is brite green. I found it when I went fishing last week. It is very friske. It would be fun to train it to do some trecks .

1. ___bright___   2. ___friske___   3. ___tricks___

4 - 5. Two periods were not put in at the ends of sentences. Correct the mistakes.

 Review

Write a word from the word list that fits each group of words.

6. mop, sweep, dust, ___broom___

7. snake, toad, pond, ___frog___

8. airplane, bus, tracks, ___train___

Spelling Words with sl and sp

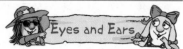
Eyes and Ears

Word List
slam
spin
speed
slip
space
slide
slick
speech
spy
sled

Sound	Spelling
/sl/	**sl**ip
/sp/	**sp**in

Say each word. Listen for the first two sounds in **slip** and **spin**.

Study the spelling. How are the first two sounds spelled?

Write the words.
1-5. Write the five words that begin with **sl**.
6-10. Write the five words that begin with **sp**.

1. slam   6. spin
2. slip   7. speed
3. slide   8. space
4. slick   9. speech
5. sled   10. spy

Spelling Tip
The /**sl**/ and /**sp**/ sounds are spelled **sl** and **sp**.

88   Spelling Words with **sl** and **sp**

Words You Know

Complete the story with the correct words from the word list.

Fun in the Winter

I love the winter. There is so much to do. When it snows, I pull my __sled__ to the top of a hill. Then I get on and __slide__ down. I pick up __speed__ going down. It feels as if I am flying through __space__.

But I must watch where I am going. At the first sign of snow, our teacher, Miss Kitty, gives the class a __speech__ on safety. We have to be careful so we do not __slam__ into a tree.

If there is no snow, I go ice skating. I like to skate on ice that is smooth and __slick__. Sometimes I __slip__ and fall. I hope no one is watching! Other times I __spin__ like a top! Then I hope my friends will __spy__ on me to see how well I skate!

Word Fun: Action Words

Slam and **spin** describe things that you can do. Circle the action word in each pair of words.

1. (talk), book   3. (smile), story   5. (sleep), cot
2. van, (drive)   4. apple, (eat)   6. food, (share)

Spelling Words with **sl** and **sp**   89

Words You Know

Seek and Find: Circle the five words from the word list hidden in the letter square. Be sure to look both across and down. Write the words in the blanks below.

c	a	s	p	i	n	t
d	e	l	o	s	p	y
s	l	i	d	e	k	m
r	s	p	e	e	c	h

1. spin
2. spy
3. slide
4. speech
5. slip

Give a Speech: Write the missing word in each title. Be sure you begin each word in the title with a capital letter.

6. How to __Spin__ a Top

7. Two ways to __Slide__ Downhill with a Sled

8. Don't __Speed__ I You'll Get There.

9. My Life as a __Spy__

Finish the Sign: Write the missing word in each sign.

Do not	55	Slow.	For Sale:	Space
Slam	mph	Road	Ice Skates	Center
the door!	Speed	Slick	and	Next
	Limit	When Wet.	Sled	Exit

90   Spelling Words with **sl** and **sp**

Word List
| slam | spin | speed | slip | space |
| slide | slick | speech | spy | sled |

Proofreading Practice

Here is Little Sister's poem. Circle the three words that are spelled wrong. Write each word correctly in the spaces below.

Ice Skating

I (slep) and (slied),
I just cannot glide.
Please give me more (spase).
So I do not fall on my face!

1. slip   2. slide   3. space

Review

Write a word from the word list for each clue below.
4. something for riding on snow   sled
5. turn around   spin
6. to watch secretly   spy

Spelling Words with **sl** and **sp**   91

150

Spelling Words that Sound Alike

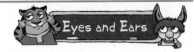
Eyes and Ears

Word List

see
sea
dear
deer
meet
meat
road
rode
dye
die

Say each word. Listen for words that sound alike.

Study the spelling. How are the words spelled? Do some words have the same sounds but different spellings and meanings?

Write the words.
1-10. Write a word. Then write a word that sounds the same. Write all ten words.

1. __see__   6. __meat__
2. __sea__   7. __road__
3. __dear__   8. __rode__
4. __deer__   9. __dye__
5. __meet__   10. __die__

Spelling Tip
Some words have the same sounds but different spellings and meanings.

92   Spelling Words that Sound Alike

Words You Know

Complete the story with the correct words from the word list.

A Trip to the Sea

Last summer I went on a trip with my grandma and grandpa. We __rode__ in their new car. We could __see__ many things along the way. We saw a little __deer__ running along the __road__. It ran right in front of our car. Luckily, we did not hit it. I was glad it did not get hurt and __die__.

Later, we stopped by the __sea__ to watch the surfers and the sailboats. Then, we got some grape popsicles. Mine melted all over my shirt. Grandma said I looked like I had purple __dye__ all over me!

That night, Mom and Dad wanted to __meet__ us for dinner. I hoped we would have pizza, but Grandpa wanted __meat__ and potatoes. At dinner, I told Mom and Dad about our trip.

Mom hugged me. "I'm glad you had such a nice day, __dear__," she said.

Word Fun: Abbreviations

Rd. is an abbreviation for **Road**. Match the correct abbreviation with each word.

Doctor   St.
Mister   Dr.
Street   Mr.
Avenue   Nov.
November   Ave.

Spelling Words that Sound Alike   93

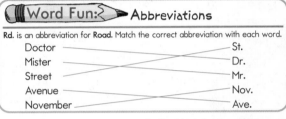
Words You Know

Look and Write: Write the words from the word list that fit each clue.

1. look at __see__
2. an ocean __sea__
3. you drive on it __road__
4. went by bus __rode__
5. someone loved __dear__
6. an animal __deer__
7. something to eat __meat__
8. come together __meet__
9. stop living __die__
10. used to color __dye__

Puzzle Play: Fill in the pair of words from the word list that fits in each puzzle. Be sure they rhyme with the word beside the puzzle.

11.
| | r | |
toad
	o	
	a	
r	o	d	e

13.
| | m | |
| | e | |
feet
| | a | |
| m | e | e | t |

15.
| | | d |
fly
| | | i |
| d | y | e |

12.
| | d | |
| | e | |
here
| | e | |
| d | e | a | r |

14. bee
	s	
s	e	e	
	a	

94   Spelling Words that Sound Alike

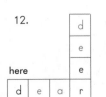

Word List
| sea | dear | meat | road | die |
| see | deer | meet | rode | dye |

Proofreading Practice

Here is Little Critter's letter. Circle the four words that are spelled wrong. Write each word correctly in the spaces below.

Dear Gator,
    I went to visit my friend Zack. I drove on a bumpy (rode). We saw a (dear). I had a great time. It was a real treat to (meat) his family. I hope I will (sea) them again soon.
            Your friend,
            Little Critter

1. __road__   2. __deer__   3. __meet__   4. __see__

Review

Write a word from the word list to fill the blank in each pair of sentences.
5. Little Critter: Look at that red bird!
   Dad: I can't __see__ it anywhere.
6. Little Sister: That dress is an ugly color.
   Mom: Why don't we __dye__ it a new color?
7. Maurice: Why is Mom's car still here?
   Molly: She __rode__ her bike to work today.

Spelling Words that Sound Alike   95

Spelling Family Names

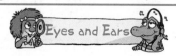
Eyes and Ears

Word List
family
mother
sister
grandmother
aunt
baby
grandfather
uncle
father
brother

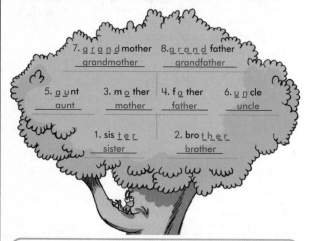

Say each word. Listen for vowel and consonant sounds you know.

Study the spelling. Look for spellings you know.

Write the words.
1-6. Write the six words that end with **er**.
7-8. Write the two words that end with long **e** spelled **y**.
9-10. Write **aunt** and **uncle**. Circle the vowels in each word.

1. mother   6. brother
2. sister   7. family
3. grandmother 8. baby
4. grandfather 9. (au)nt
5. father   10. (u)ncl(e)

Spelling Tip
Some family names have spellings you know.
Others have spellings that must be remembered.

Words You Know

Complete the story with the correct words from the word list.

My Family

My name is Maurice. I have a large __family__. I have a twin __sister__ named Molly. I call my __mother__ Mom, and I call my __father__ Dad. Someday, I hope my mother has another __baby__. I want a little __brother__!

My mother's sister is my __aunt__. My mother's mother is my __grandmother__. I like when they come to Critterville to visit. They always tell funny stories about Mom.

My father's brother is my __uncle__. My father's father is my __grandfather__. They take Molly and me fishing every summer. I love my family!

Word Fun: Pronouns

Write each sentence using **He**, **She**, **They**, or **We** in place of the underlined words.
1. My mother will sing.   She will sing
2. You and I can go.   We can go.
3. Our sister and brother ski.   They ski.
4. His uncle works at home.   He works at home.
5. Her grandmother has a cat.   She has a cat.

Words You Know

Map the Family: Fill in the missing letters. Then write the words that are spelled.

7. g r a n d mother   8. g r a n d father
   grandmother   grandfather

5. a u nt   3. m o ther   4. f a ther   6. u n cle
   aunt   mother   father   uncle

1. sis t e r   2. bro t h e r
   sister   brother

Meet the Family: Write the words from the word list that fit each clue.

9. mom's sister	aunt	13. boy child	brother
10. dad's brother	uncle	14. girl child	sister
11. dad's mother	grandmother	15. all of the people	family
12. mom's father	grandfather	16. very young child	baby

Word List
family	mother	brother	aunt
baby	father	sister	uncle
grandfather		grandmother	

Proofreading Practice

Here is Bun Bun's description of a family member. Circle the four words that are spelled wrong. Write each word correctly in the spaces below.

Why is my (ant) so special? She is the one in my (famly) who can do everything. She can fix a car. She is a great cook. She tells funny stories to my (broter) and (sistre).

1. aunt   2. family   3. brother   4. sister

5. One question mark was not put at the end of a question. Correct the mistake.

Review

Write a word from the word list that goes with each word below as in the example.
grandmother - grandfather

6. mother –   father

7. sister –   brother

8. aunt –   uncle

Spelling the / u̇/ Sound

Eyes and Ears

Sound	Spelling
/u̇/	push hook

Word List

put
hook
full
took
push
foot
book
pull
look
good

Say each word. Listen for the vowel sound you hear in **push** and **hook**. Note the sign for this sound.

Study the spelling. How is the vowel sound spelled in each word?

Write the words.
1-10. Write the ten words. Circle the letter that spells the /u̇/ sound.

1. p(u)t   6. f(oo)t
2. h(oo)k   7. b(oo)k
3. f(u)ll   8. p(u)ll
4. t(oo)k   9. l(oo)k
5. p(u)sh   10. g(oo)d

◎ Spelling Tip
The vowel sound /u̇/ maybe spelled u or oo.

Words You Know

Complete the story with the correct words from the word list.

Another Fish Story

Malcolm wanted to learn how to fish. So he went to the library to __look__ for a __book__. The shelves were __full__ of all kinds of books. He soon found a guide to fishing that looked as if it would be __good__. He __took__ it out.

The book told Malcolm everything he ever wanted to know about fishing. He even learned how to tie the __hook__ to the fishing line.

One day, Malcolm got into a rowboat for the first time. He did not even know where to __put__ each __foot__. He started to __pull__ the oars toward him and then __push__ them away. But the boat did not move. Malcolm will have to read another book!

✎ Word Fun: More Than One

Write the plurals of the underlined words below. Use the words in the word box.

men	feet	children	mice

1. one <u>foot</u>, two __feet__   3. one <u>child</u>, two __children__
2. one <u>man</u>, two __men__   4. one <u>mouse</u>, two __mice__

Words You Know

Dial a Word: Turn the letters on the dial to write four words.

1. __book__
2. __hook__
3. __look__
4. __took__

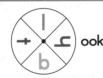
ook

Change the Meaning: Write the words that are the opposites of the underlined words.

5. The apple tasted <u>bad</u>.
   __good__
6. Who <u>gave</u> these books?
   __took__
7. My glass is <u>empty</u>.
   __full__
8. Will you <u>push</u> the cart?
   __pull__

Write a Rhyme: Write the words that finish the rhymes.

9. "After I fix supper," said the cook.
   "I will read a good __book__."
10. I sat for a while by the brook.
    Then I put some bait on my __hook__.
11. I know for sure that is the crook!
    I got a very close __look__.
12. It is a shopping cart, not a rose bush.
    Please help me and give it a __push__.
13. I need a place for my left foot.
    Where do you think it can be __put__?
14. The chimney was full of soot.
    When I tried to clean it, soot dropped on my __foot__.

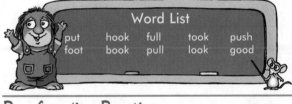
Word List

| put | hook | full | took | push |
| foot | book | pull | look | good |

Proofreading Practice

Here is Gabby's book report. Circle the three words that are spelled wrong. Write each word correctly in the spaces below.

<u>Amelia Bedelia</u> is a funny (buk). Amelia is a (gud) cook, but she gets things mixed up. She (poot) bows on a chicken. She took some lightbulbs outside and hung them on a clothesline. I would like her as a friend!

1. __book__   2. __good__   3. __put__

🌐 Review

Write a word from the word list to finish each sentence. The missing word will rhyme with the underlined word.

4. A nice log is __good__ <u>wood</u>.

5. To press on a little tree is to __push__ a <u>bush</u>.

6. At the library you <u>look</u> for a __book__.

Spelling the /ou/ Sound

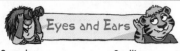
Eyes and Ears

Sound	Spelling
/ou/	town sound

Word List
- out
- now
- clown
- our
- down
- sound
- owl
- house
- town
- loud

Say each word. Listen for the vowel sound in **town** and **sound**.

Study the spelling. How is the /ou/ sound spelled in each word?

Write the words.
1–10. Write the ten words. Circle the letters that spell the /ou/ sound.

1. (ou)t
2. n(ow)
3. cl(ow)n
4. (ou)r
5. d(ow)n

6. s(ou)nd
7. (ow)l
8. h(ou)se
9. t(ow)n
10. l(ou)d

> **Spelling Tip**
> The /ou/ sound may be spelled **ow** and **ou**.

Words You Know

Complete the story with the correct words from the word list.

The Circus

Listen, everybody! The circus has come to __town__. You do not have to leave your __house__ to buy tickets for the show. Call right __now__. Bring the whole family.

You will laugh at a funny __clown__ riding on a horse. You will see two acrobats shot __out__ of a cannon. Then they will come __down__ in a net. Just remember to block your ears. The __sound__ of the cannon blast is very __loud__! You will see __our__ amazing skywalkers cross the wire.

You can come to the circus during the day. Or, you can come in the evening if you are a night __owl__. Do not delay! Call today!

> **Word Fun:** Words That Tell When
>
> Now tells when something is happening. Circle the word in each pair that tells **when**.
> 1. (today), town
> 2. newspaper, (never)
> 3. (always), apple
> 4. (sometimes), sun
> 5. talk, (tomorrow)
> 6. (yesterday), yawn

Words You Know

Look and Write: Write the words from the word list that have the same ending sounds as the picture names.

 nut
 hand
sled
 mouse

1. __out__
3. __sound__
5. __loud__
7. __house__

 cow
flower
towel
crown

2. __now__
4. __our__
6. __owl__
8. __clown__
9. __down__
10. __town__

Rhyme and Write: Finish the sentences with words that rhyme with the underlined words.

11. A person who is sad in the circus is a <u>frown</u> __clown__ .
12. A bird on something you dry with is an __owl__ <u>towel</u>.
13. A little creature in your home is a <u>house</u> __mouse__.

Finish the News: Write the missing word from the word list that finishes the newspaper headline. Be sure to begin each word with a capital letter.

14. The Circus is Coming to __Town__
15. __Loud__ Rocket Blasts Off!
16. Car Runs __Out__ of Gas on Highway

Word List

sound	now	clown	our	down
out	owl	house	town	loud

Proofreading Practice

Here is Little Sister's list. Circle the three words that are spelled wrong. Write each word correctly in the spaces below.

Ways to Make Your Friends Laugh
1. Make a funny (sownd).
2. Say up when you mean down.
3. Dress up like a (cloun).
4. Hoot like an (oul).
5. Draw a silly picture of your brother.

1. __sound__   2. __clown__   3. __owl__

> ## Review
>
> Write a word from the word list that means the same as each underlined part of the poems below.
>
> 4. "This is the <u>home</u> that Jack built." __house__
> — Nursery Rhyme
> 5. "Jack fell <u>from a higher to a lower place</u> and broke his crown." __down__   — Nursery Rhyme
> 6. "The <u>bird with large staring eyes</u> and the Pussy-Cat went to sea." __owl__   — Edward Lear

Spelling Compound Words

Eyes and Ears

Word + Word = Compound Word
dog + house = doghouse

Word List
maybe
bedroom
lunchroom
into
something
nobody
doghouse
myself
inside
notebook

Say each word. Listen for the two words you hear in each word.

Study the spelling. Look for familiar words in each word. How many words do you see in each word?

Write the words.
1-10. Write the ten words. Circle each of the words that you find in the compound words.

1. (may)(be)   6. (no)(body)
2. (bed)(room)   7. (dog)(house)
3. (lunch)(room)   8. (my)(self)
4. (in)(to)   9. (in)(side)
5. (some)(thing)   10. (note)(book)

Spelling Tip
◎ Compound words are formed by joining two other words.

108   Spelling Compound Words

Words You Know

Complete the story with the correct words from the word list.

School Days

On school days I get up very early. There is __nobody__ else up at this hour. I stay in my __bedroom__ and read for a while. Then I get dressed all by __myself__.

Before I leave, I always have __something__ to eat. Sometimes I have toast, or __maybe__ some cereal. While I eat, I hear scratching on the door. It is my dog, Blue. He sleeps in a __doghouse__ in our yard at night. I open the door and let him __inside__.

When it is time to leave, I get my things together. I check to make sure I have my pencil and __notebook__. Most days I put my lunch __into__ my backpack. Sometimes I like to buy lunch at school. Everyone in my class eats in the __lunchroom__. At the door, I pat Blue and off I go!

Word Fun: Words That Tell Where

Inside tells where something happened. Circle the word in each pair that tells where.
1. (out,) every   4. (upstairs,) something
2. with, (below)   5. smart, (around)
3. full, (down)   6. (across,) first

Spelling Compound Words   109

Words You Know

Put the Pieces Together: Write the words from the word list that are spelled by fitting the pieces of the puzzles together. Only use each piece once.

may   self   some   book
in   my   thing
note side   be

1. __maybe__
2. __something__
3. __myself__
4. __inside__
5. __notebook__

Join the Words: Write the words that are made by joining two words in each sentence into a compound word. Use the word list to help you.

6. I will eat my lunch in my room today.   __lunchroom__
7. Did you find a note in your spelling book? __notebook__
8. You may fall on the steps, so please be careful. __maybe__
9. My dog likes to stay in the house at night. __doghouse__
10 Make the bed in your room before you leave. __bedroom__
11. There are no bones in the body of a worm. __nobody__
12. Take the box in the kitchen to the shed. __into__

110   Spelling Compound Words

Word List
maybe   bedroom   myself   notebook
nobody doghouse into   inside
lunchroom   something

Proofreading Practice

Here is Gator's description. Circle the three words that are spelled wrong. Write each word correctly in the spaces below.

I walked to school by (miself.) It rained all day so we stayed inside for recess. We ate in the new (lunchrum.) Our teacher gave us a spelling (notbook.) I made a new friend. I was busy so the day passed by very quickly.

1. __myself__   2. __lunchroom__   3. __notebook__

4-5. Two periods were not put at the ends of sentences. Correct the mistakes.

Review

Write a word from the word list for each clue below.

6. It is where you eat at school.   __lunchroom__
7. You write things in it.   __notebook__
6. You say this instead of **yes** or **no**.   __maybe__

Spelling Compound Words   111

155

Spelling Number Words

Eyes and Ears

Word List

one
two
three
four
five
six
seven
eight
nine
ten

Say each word. Listen for familiar vowel and consonant sounds.

Study the spelling. Do you see some short and long vowel spellings you have studied? Do you see any unusual spellings?

Write the words.
1-10. Write the ten words. Circle the short and long vowel spellings you see.

1. (o)ne
2. two
3. thr(ee)
4. four
5. f(i)v(e)

6. s(i)x
7. s(e)ven
8. (eigh)t
9. n(i)n(e)
10. t(e)n

Spelling Tip
Some number words have common spellings. Others must be remembered.

Words You Know

Complete the story with the correct words from the word list.

Just the Numbers, Please
Ten students in Miss Kitty's class were divided into two teams. Five children were on each team.
Here are the ten math problems they had to solve:

Two plus five is   seven .
Three plus five is   eight .
Six minus four is   two .
Seven minus six is   one .
Four plus six is   ten .
Nine minus four is   five .
Three plus one is   four .
Eight minus five is   three .
Two plus four is   six .
Six plus three is   nine .

Each student had to give the answer to one problem. How many would you have gotten right? Would you have helped your team to win?

Word Fun: Homophones

Some number words are **homophones**. Homophones are words that sound alike but are spelled differently. Write the word with the correct spelling and meaning to complete each sentence.

1. I go to school. (to, two)
2. Here is one hat. (one, won)
3. We ate lunch. (eight, ate)
4. Pass four cups. (for, four)

Words You Know

Look and Count: Write the word from the word list that tells how many of each thing listed below you find in the picture.

1. three balls
2. two clocks
3. four pictures
4. seven books
5. one fish

Tell How Many: Write the words from the word list that answer the questions.

6. How many fingers are on one hand?   five
7. How many toes are on both feet?   ten
8. How many ears does a dog have?   two
9. How many sides are in a △?   three
10. How many noses are on one face?   one
11. How many people are in two pairs of twins? four
12. How many days are in one week?   seven
13. How many letters are in the word **classroom**? nine
14. What is six plus two?   eight

Word List
one   three   five   seven   nine
two   four   six   eight   ten

Proofreading Practice

Here is Little Critter's story. Circle the three words that are spelled wrong. Write each word correctly in the spaces below.

My name is Little Critter. I am (sevin) years old. I am in the second grade. I love animals. I have (for) pets. I have (won) dog. I have a cat and a frog. I also have a goldfish. When I am eight years old, I will get a new pet. I hope it is a horse!

1. seven
2. four
3. one

Review
Write a word from the word list to anwer each question using the pictures.

4. How many teeth?
   two
5. How many legs?
   eight
6. How many sides?
   four

NOTES

NOTES

NOTES

NOTES